NORTH CAROLINA TAR HEELS

Where Have You Gone?

SCOTT FOWLER

FOREWORD BY
WOODY DURHAM

www.SportsPublishingLLC.com

ISBN: 1-58261-942-5

Publishers: Peter L. Bannon and Joseph J. Bannon Sr.
Senior managing editor: Susan M. Moyer
Acquisitions editor: Mike Pearson
Developmental editor: Doug Hoepker
Art director: K. Jeffrey Higgerson
Dust jacket design: Joseph T. Brumleve
Interior layout: Kathryn R. Holleman
Imaging: Kathryn R. Holleman, Dustin Hubbart, and Heidi Norsen
Photo editor: Erin Linden-Levy
Media and promotions managers: Kelley Brown (regional),
        Randy Fouts (national), Maurey Williamson (print)

Printed in the United States of America

Sports Publishing L.L.C.
804 North Neil Street
Champaign, IL 61820

Phone: 1-877-424-2665
Fax: 217-363-2073
www.SportsPublishingLLC.com

*To my own wonderful family—my wife, Elise, and our boys,
Chapel, Salem, and London.*

*And to the Carolina family—all 35 of the North Carolina basketball
players who allowed me into their lives so that
this book could be possible.*

CONTENTS

FOREWORD

By Woody Durham
UNC CLASS OF 1963
RADIO "VOICE OF THE TAR HEELS" SINCE 1971

I admit it. I am extremely fortunate. In the spring of 1971, I got an opportunity to do something that would define my career in broadcasting. Since then, I've broadcast more than 1,500 Carolina football and basketball games on the radio. That's better than 1,100 Tar Heel basketball games.

And you know what? I still love it. I still get a little nervous before every game, especially the big ones. I still get a rush of adrenaline with the opening tip or a dramatic last shot.

So much of the credit for the excitement and the tradition of nearly 100 years of Carolina basketball belongs to Dean Smith. It was a thrill to be associated with him for most of the 1,133 games he coached at Carolina, and I learned so much more than just basketball from him. Any credit for his success was always passed along to his players.

That's why this book by Scott Fowler is such a great idea. It describes the success of Carolina basketball by emphasizing the contribution of the players, both during their time in Chapel Hill and in their lives since then. *North Carolina Tar Heels: Where Have You Gone?* is a book you will want to read, and a book you will want to keep.

Compared to some people, I came to Carolina basketball a little late. Growing up in North Carolina, I was first a fan of Carolina football. We lived in Mebane. When my father, Dallas Durham, returned from World War II, my parents bought football season tickets to see the teams of the fabulous Charlie Justice era. Later in life, my wife, Jean, and I became friends with Charlie and Sarah Justice and with so many of the other players on those teams.

Like a lot of other people at that time, I came to Carolina basketball during the perfect 32-0 season of 1957. What excitement! What tension! Ten games decided by eight points or less! That national championship really was "Frank McGuire's Miracle."

My dad was in the textile business, and by 1957 we had moved from Mebane to Mount Holly and then to Albemarle. I can tell you exactly where I was and who I was with watching the two 1957 Final Four games from Kansas City. On

Since 1971, the man all Carolina basketball fans know simply as "Woody" has broadcast more than 1,100 UNC basketball games.

Friday night for the first triple overtime game in the national semifinals against Michigan State, I was at a friend's house in Albemarle. Then Saturday night for the championship game against Kansas, my dad and I were on the edge of our seats in our own den. Many of the 1957 players later became close friends of mine, and Scott Fowler has devoted the first four chapters of this book to some of the outstanding players on that squad.

C.D. Chesley put those Kansas City games on television across North Carolina, and in 1958, with the support of the Pilot Life Insurance Company in Greensboro, he produced the *ACC Basketball Game of the Week*. Can you believe there was only one ACC game a week on TV?

I got my first job in radio, WZKY in Albemarle, a week before my 16th birthday. But when I enrolled at Carolina in 1959, I was interested in a television career. I worked part-time at WUNC-TV and was fortunate to be on the Chesley crew for numerous ACC games. He even gave me the opportunity to announce some games on the Saturdays when he split his network coverage.

Later, while serving as the Sports Director of WFMY-TV in Greensboro, I worked the ACC games on television for four years with Jim Thacker, Bones McKinney, and Bobby Roberts.

In 1971, Carolina was looking for a new radio play-by-play broadcaster. Charlotte's Bill Currie left in February to take a new TV job in Pittsburgh, and Bob Lamey, who worked with Currie at WSOC radio and TV, stepped in to finish the season. Homer Rice, then the UNC Athletic Director, discovered I was a Carolina graduate. So he contacted me to gauge my interest.

Doing the games on radio was not even on my radar. But I had grown up a Tar Heel fan, I had gone to school in Chapel Hill, and so I became interested. Bill Dooley and Dean Smith gave me their support, and I got the opportunity for a career-altering assignment. Twenty-five years later, Rice was the AD at Georgia Tech when he hired my oldest son, Wes, to broadcast football and basketball games for the Yellow Jackets. Gosh, isn't it funny how some things work out?

My first year as "Voice of the Tar Heels" was 1971-72. Carolina made it to the Final Four in Los Angeles. It was the fourth trip in six years for a Dean Smith team, and I remember thinking, "Hey, this is great! We'll probably go to the Final Four every year!" Of course, the Tar Heels didn't get back until 1977 in Atlanta.

However, while broadcasting the Tar Heels, I have followed them to 11 different Final Fours. That includes the 2005 Final Four in St. Louis, when UNC defeated Michigan State and Illinois to win the national championship.

I have described every play as they won or shared 15 regular-season crowns in the competitive ACC. The Tar Heels have also captured 11 ACC Tournament titles. Four different times they finished the season as the nation's top-ranked team. And, of course, Carolina has won three national championships while I have been broadcasting the team's games—in 1982, 1993 and 2005.

During my time behind the mike—and I hope I have a few more years left—168 players have been a part of Carolina basketball. Forty-six were chosen All-ACC. Another 33 were honored with various All-America awards, and six were singled out as National Players of the Year. More than 60 were drafted to play professional basketball, and more than a dozen of those left the program a year or two early. Think what might have happened to Carolina basketball if all of the lottery picks had not followed Coach Smith's recommendation to go pro.

Coach Smith always maintained that during the season he did what was best for the team. After the season, he did what was best for the players. I think the players chronicled in this book recognized his philosophy and learned from it. Then they applied it to their own lives and careers after basketball.

When the Dean E. Smith Center was built in the 1980s, Coach Smith did not want his name on it. Instead, he wanted his players to be honored, but there was no way to put numerous individual names on the building. So he finally agreed to name it the Dean E. Smith Student Activities Center, but he has always referred to it as simply the "Student Activities Center." I can assure you he doesn't like hearing it called the "Dean Dome."

The 2005-06 campaign will be my 35th season broadcasting Carolina basketball games. During the fall of 2005 I will work my 400th football game, and I've also had a lot of thrills following those teams. Hopefully, we'll continue to have more fun in the near future following both sports.

Some fans think Carolina basketball is all the way back. But it's not quite where Roy Williams wants it to be, even though he won his first national title with the 2005 Tar Heels. Coach Williams continues to strive for the consistent success that the program enjoyed under the leadership of both Dean Smith and Bill Guthridge, and I want to help him in any way I can.

The former players also stand ready to offer their support. Their time in Chapel Hill was a unique experience, and their success is really the story of an outstanding basketball program at a special public university. Those players have interesting and diverse stories to tell about their careers and their lives. That's why I'm so glad Scott Fowler has put together *North Carolina Tar Heels: Where Have You Gone?*

Now you can enjoy some of those stories, too.

INTRODUCTION

By Scott Fowler

This book isn't about Michael Jordan. You already know what happened to him. It's not about North Carolina's 2005 national championship team. We don't know yet what will ultimately happen to all of those outstanding players. This book is about 35 other men who also wore Carolina blue—and what happened after they took their jerseys off for the last time.

Some of the men whose lives are chronicled in *North Carolina Tar Heels: Where Have You Gone?* were superstars in Chapel Hill—men like Phil Ford, Billy Cunningham, Larry Miller, Al Wood, and Charlie Scott. Some of them also won national championships, like Eric Montross and Lennie Rosenbluth. Some of them barely played at all at UNC but became major successes in other fields—doctors, dentists, bank presidents, teachers, and ministers.

All of them have both a public and private history. If you're a Tar Heel fan, you know part of it—the public record of the basketball games they won and lost during their time at UNC. But you don't know about their personal hardships, their families, and their triumphs. You don't know which one had his NBA career ended by a baby gate. Or which one became the CEO of the second largest bank in the world. Or which one came to the North Carolina basketball reunion in February 2004 just two months after a brain aneurysm nearly killed him.

All of these former players trusted me and let me into their lives to allow me to tell their stories, and for that I will always be grateful. It undoubtedly helped that I am a North Carolina alumnus myself (Class of 1987), as well as a former sports editor at *The Daily Tar Heel*, the excellent campus newspaper at UNC. Like all of these men, I treasured my own college experience at Chapel Hill. My real job now is sports columnist for *The Charlotte Observer*, where I have worked since 1994 writing four columns a week on all sports topics.

This book contains 35 chapters, each focusing on a different former Tar Heel basketball player. The cornerstone of each and every chapter: my in-depth interview with the player himself. I decided early in this project to only write about players who were: 1) alive; 2) extremely interesting from a journalistic standpoint; and 3) totally willing to cooperate.

The cooperation part turned out to be a little easier than I thought. Every player I was able to find and speak with directly was happy to have his story included as part of this book—and to grant the detailed interview necessary to make that happen. About half of my interviews with these players were done on the phone (mostly the players who live out of state). The others were conducted in person.

Among many other notable experiences, this book afforded me the chance to eat pancakes at an IHOP with Al Wood; talk with Tom LaGarde in his old dairy barn now filled with vintage wood; watch a UNC-Wake Forest basketball game on TV with Brian Reese; spend most of a day in Asheville with Joseph Forte; get tricked by a prank call from Steve Previs; tour principal Lee Dedmon's excellent high school in Gastonia; visit Charlie Shaffer in Atlanta at his extraordinary Marcus Institute; and marvel at the sanctuary of Charlotte's innovative Forest Hill Church with pastor David Chadwick.

Dozens more former UNC players could have been included in this book, and it's almost certain that a few of your favorite players have been left out. Sorry about that.

I tried to choose a representative sampling from each decade, starting with the 1950s. But I also wanted to keep the number of chapters somewhat manageable, so I could write longer, more revealing stories about each man. I chose not to write about current NBA all-stars with UNC pedigrees, since all you have to do to find out where Antawn Jamison, Rasheed Wallace, Vince Carter, and Jerry Stackhouse are right now is to check the NBA schedule in today's newspaper. I also tried to select a variety of players, from UNC's all-time leading scorer Phil Ford (2,290 points—Chapter 22) to former Charlotte mayor Richard Vinroot (exactly one point—Chapter 7).

I was also able to interview former North Carolina coaches Dean Smith and Bill Guthridge at considerable length about many of the players in this book, and I so much appreciate their time. Coach Smith turned 74 in 2005. Once in our interview he joked about having a "senior moment," but don't let him fool you. Smith's legendary memory is still virtually photographic. In his familiar nasal twang, Smith rattled off the names of his former players' wives and children, along with recent tidbits about their current jobs and successes, throughout our interview.

"All of my players are so special to me," Smith said several times. I hope that all of our own children some day have a teacher who cares as much about his pupils as Smith always has and still does.

Smith rarely does interviews anymore. But he agreed to do this one once he understood that this book was about his players, not him, and that each former player in the book had given the okay.

Woody Durham, the radio "Voice of the Tar Heels" since 1971, not only contributed a wonderful foreword to this book but also helped me more fully understand each player and his career at Carolina.

And Roy Williams, current coach of the Tar Heels and now the proud owner of his own national championship, gave me a better idea of why so many of these players have obtained leadership positions after leaving Chapel Hill.

"Think of the self-sacrifice involved in playing basketball at Carolina," Williams said. "Think of the discipline. Think of the work—the willingness these players had, to spend extra time at something to try and push themselves past the place where they thought they could go. All of that correlates to life after basketball."

As anyone who went to Carolina knows—or any ACC basketball fan, for that matter—the Tar Heel basketball program is extraordinary. Not just because of Dean Smith's all-time record of 879 career wins, or because of the school's four national championships and NCAA-record 16 Final Fours. But because everyone *cares* so much.

Said Scott Williams (Chapter 28), who survived a terrible family tragedy during his UNC career in the late 1980s and went on to a 15-year NBA career: "I never thought the coaches cared more about the wins and losses as they did about us growing up to be good citizens and people who could be counted on by society. Everyone I talk to—Mitch Kupchak, Bob McAdoo, Larry Brown, George Karl, guys from every generation—it's always, 'Hey, what's up, Carolina?' We all share this common experience that will bond us forever."

Said Steve Previs (Chapter 17), a guard in the early 1970s for the Tar Heels: "Look at the list of alumni from this program—99 percent turn out to be leaders of some kind. Now Dean Smith will take no credit for that, but it all started with him. I can't tell you how deeply indebted I am to him and to the program. My greatest nightmare, literally, used to be waking up and finding out that I'd gone to some other school and passed up my Carolina experience. That still makes me shiver."

Longtime ESPN basketball announcer Dick Vitale has noted that players from North Carolina frequently do something notable in their lives long after Chapel Hill is just a memory. "So often," Vitale said, "sports can help the transition to real life. Athletes understand sweat. And pain. And joy."

Continued Vitale: "I have a problem with guys at other programs who say all they care about is basketball. Look, they can be Michael Jordan. They can be Larry Bird. But at some point, they are still going to be sitting at a press conference, in front of a lot of cameras, and saying goodbye. It's over. They still have to live their lives between ages 35 and 85. And what are they going to do? Life isn't a golf course. You have to do something productive. And the guys at Carolina always got a head start because of that program."

The players chronicled in this book have made many fine contributions as coaches. And cardiologists. And city councilmen. And on and on. They have also continued to support and love their alma mater.

Said Vinroot: "Much as I know everyone loves their university, I don't know of any feeling quite as powerful as that a Carolina person has for Chapel Hill."

Smith and Guthridge will take no credit for all this, although the players try their best to shovel it toward them.

"Don't try to make it like we were the reason these guys did all this," Smith said at the beginning of our interview for this book. "The players were the reason. I owe them all so much."

Said Guthridge: "First of all, these guys were good people when we recruited them. Most everybody we recruited came from good families. They were good students. I don't think we can take credit for making them very successful. I do think they enjoyed our program and enjoyed the discipline we had and the way Coach Smith coached. Almost all of them got their degrees, and we're really proud of what they have accomplished."

The number "35" is significant to this book, and not just because that's the number of players I interviewed. The actual jersey number "35" is also symbolic of the book's approach. It was worn at Carolina by four of my interview subjects (Pete Brennan, Lee Dedmon, Bob McAdoo and Dave Popson). The number has been "honored" twice by UNC officials, due to the considerable accomplishments of McAdoo and Doug Moe, and so it hangs in the Smith Center rafters.

But the number has not been retired. It continues to be used today, much like I hope the 35 chapters of this book will continue to be read for years to come by Tar Heel fans who wonder whatever happened to their heroes once the cheering stopped.

LENNIE ROSENBLUTH

The MVP of 32-0

If you are a North Carolina basketball fan, you've undoubtedly heard the true story about the time Michael Jordan was cut from his high-school basketball team in Wilmington, N.C. That happened to Lennie Rosenbluth, too.

Twice.

Rosenbluth ultimately became the star player on North Carolina's 1957 national championship team, averaging 28 points on a squad that went 32-0 and edged Wilt Chamberlain's Kansas squad in triple overtime in the NCAA final. Rosenbluth, now 72, remains the closest thing North Carolina basketball ever had to Tar Heel football legend Charlie "Choo Choo" Justice. Both were stars in the pre-television era, both were remembered for decades in Chapel Hill for their accomplishments, and both had very modest pro careers.

Rosenbluth played only two years in the NBA before ultimately settling in Miami with his wife and two children. The Rosenbluths moved to Miami in 1965 and never left. Rosenbluth taught U.S. history and social studies and coached basketball at both public and private schools in the area. He ran the same system his old college coach, Frank McGuire, did for years in Miami. And he liked to quote McGuire occasionally to his teams.

"Frank McGuire always said the basketball was gold, and you never throw away gold," Rosenbluth would preach.

The best player Rosenbluth ever coached? A young Chris Corchiani, who would later star at N.C. State.

Rosenbluth ultimately coached more than 20 years of basketball, mostly at the high school level, and taught for close to 30. He and his wife had two children, Steve and Elizabeth, who have since supplied them with six grandkids. Long before all that, though, Rosenbluth was a New York kid growing up in The

LENNIE ROSENBLUTH

1955-1957

Lennie Rosenbluth (above) averaged 28 points a game for UNC's 1957 championship team that went undefeated. In 2004, Rosenbluth (right) appeared at the UNC Letterman's Reunion banquet, and referred to himself during his speech as "Lennie 'Shoot-a-Lot' Rosenbluth." Today, he lives in Miami and has been retired from coaching and teaching for ten years.

Bronx who didn't start playing basketball until seventh grade and admittedly wasn't much good at the sport for years.

In 10th grade, Rosenbluth went out for the varsity squad—and was cut.

"I not only wasn't good enough to make the varsity," Rosenbluth said, "I didn't even make the junior varsity team."

As a junior, Rosenbluth tried to make his New York high school team—and failed again.

But Rosenbluth's story is a testament to perseverance. He kept playing in various leagues outside of high school, developing his body and his game. Eventually, he was noticed by everyone.

As a kid in New York City, Rosenbluth had a number of quintessential New York experiences. He played lots of stickball in the street. And he remembers going to nearby Yankee games and sitting in the bleachers for 50 cents.

"I'd take a buck," Rosenbluth said, "and pack a lunch. The subway was a nickel. A scorecard was a dime. You still had money left over for drinks. For a buck, you could be there all day."

When Rosenbluth finally made his high-school team as a senior, he got to play a couple of games in Madison Square Garden. That led to a summer job at a hotel in the Catskills, where Rosenbluth would work some in the day and play basketball at night for the hotel team. All the resorts in the Catskills at the time had their own basketball teams, as they were a cheap way to provide occasional entertainment for the guests.

In the Catskills, after his senior year, Rosenbluth's game finally took off. A 6-5, 175-pound forward, he had a knack for scoring from anywhere. After never scoring more than 18 points in any one game in high school, he started getting 25 or 30 every night.

"The one thing I really always had was that just about any shot I would work on, I'd end up mastering it," Rosenbluth said. "I had a two-hand outside set shot, a one-hand push shot, a hook shot, and I got the ball off very quickly. If one man guarded me alone, he'd end up fouling out."

Red Auerbach, the legendary Boston Celtics coach, was moonlighting as a summer-league coach at one of the resorts. He liked Rosenbluth so much that he invited him to work out with the Celtics, giving Rosenbluth the impression he might be able to make the jump straight from high school to the pros. NBA officials told Auerbach that couldn't happen, so Rosenbluth needed to find a college. He was also going to need to attend prep school for a year since he lacked some of the necessary entrance requirements.

A talent scout named Harry Gotkin had befriended Rosenbluth and helped arrange his college recruitment. After meeting N.C. State coach Everett Case in New York and working out for him, Rosenbluth said he was "basically offered a scholarship."

"In April 1952, Coach' Case invited me down to look at the campus in Raleigh," Rosenbluth said. "Then, before I know it, there are 100 kids in the gym. For me, it was hot. I'm completely out of shape and can hardly run the court without breathing heavily. It turns out to be a tryout, and at the end, Case tells me, 'I have only one scholarship available. I know I talked to you about it, but I can't use you. I can't waste the scholarship.'"

Gotkin re-entered the picture. Gotkin was also a good friend and an unofficial talent scout for McGuire, the dapper basketball coach who in early 1952 was still the head coach at his alma mater, St. John's. Gotkin told Rosenbluth that McGuire was about to leave St. John's and would be willing to give Rosenbluth a scholarship wherever the coach went.

"This was despite the fact McGuire had never seen me play," Rosenbluth said.

McGuire went to North Carolina, taking over the program in 1952. In the fall of 1953, after his prep-school year, Rosenbluth arrived in Chapel Hill.

Rosenbluth gave a speech at the North Carolina basketball reunion banquet in February 2004 that recalled the culture shock he felt when first arriving in Chapel Hill. He didn't know what grits or black-eyed peas were. And he noticed everyone seemed to have a middle name, like "Jim Bob."

"So I said I was Lennie 'Shoot-a-Lot' Rosenbluth," he said, breaking up the crowd in laughter.

Rosenbluth played on the freshman team in 1953-54 and started to light it up, but few people actually saw what he was doing at first.

"We started out playing in front of no more than 100 people in Woollen Gym for a lot of those freshman games," Rosenbluth said. "For our first game, the coach gave us a pep talk, we ran up the stairs, ready to go—and the gym was locked. There was nobody in the place."

But word got around about the skinny New Yorker who lived in Joyner dorm and could shoot like crazy. By the end of his freshman year, the crowds had increased 10-fold for Rosenbluth's freshman games. And by the time he was a sophomore, McGuire knew he had a future star. Rosenbluth averaged 25.5 points as a sophomore, 26.7 as a junior and then 28 as a senior at North Carolina. He still holds the Tar Heel records for single-season and career scoring average (26.9). His old No.10 is one of the seven retired numbers in UNC history.

"I had absolutely great teammates," Rosenbluth said. "They were all from New York, too. They all bought into feeding me the ball, which they didn't have to do."

In 1957, the Tar Heels merged into one of the greatest teams ever. Point guard Tommy Kearns, forward Pete Brennan, center Joe Quigg, forward Bobby Cunningham and the rest spanked one team after another on the way to the NCAA Final Four, which they entered with a 30-0 record. Rosenbluth was the lone Jewish player among the starters—the rest were Catholic—which was duly noted in one newspaper story after another of the period.

That Final Four, played in Kansas City, was notable for several things. North Carolina won both of its games in triple overtime, against Michigan State in the semifinals, 74-70, and against Kansas and Chamberlain in the finals, 54-53.

"Coach McGuire did a very smart thing before the final against Kansas," Rosenbluth said. "He went up to each player and asked him, 'Are you afraid of Chamberlain?' We'd all say 'No,' of course. But he told us, 'Kansas cannot beat you. Chamberlain can, but Kansas can't. We're going to take the gamble and let anyone besides Chamberlain shoot.'"

Playing the sort of stacked defense that NBA teams now often employ against Shaquille O'Neal and using a very deliberate offense, the Tar Heels held Chamberlain to 23 points and 14 rebounds in their one-point win on March 23, 1957. Rosenbluth fouled out after scoring 20 points and wasn't on the court at the end. But his team ultimately won the championship, and Rosenbluth was named the collegiate player of the year over Chamberlain.

Those collegiate moments turned out to be the finest of Rosenbluth's career. And 1957—the year he set the UNC scoring record of 895 points that still stands—remains one of the highlights of his life. He also got married that year, to his college sweetheart, the former Pat Oliver of Mt. Airy, North Carolina.

"But in the NBA, I got drafted by the wrong team," he explained. "The Philadelphia Warriors took me, and they already had a 6-5 guy who did the same things I did."

That guy was Paul Arizin, who would eventually wind up in the Basketball Hall of Fame.

Unaccustomed to being a backup, Rosenbluth played in the NBA for only two unhappy seasons.

"I only played when Arizin was out, and he didn't sit down much," Rosenbluth said. "The NBA money was nowhere like it was today—I think the average salary was between $5,000-$7,000 a year. We had no trainers. And the travel was hard. We used to fly on newspaper runs at night, on the same planes that were delivering newspapers up and down the East Coast."

When the Warriors decided they would hold preseason practice in California their third season, Rosenbluth decided he didn't want to go to the West Coast to practice and instead retired. He came back to Chapel Hill, managed a bowling alley and also headed back to school to obtain his teacher's certificate. Rosenbluth's first teaching job was in Wilson, North Carolina.

The first basketball team he coached lost every single game. His second season as a coach was better. At some point, he ran across a recruiter from Miami who wanted new teachers to move there.

"My salary was $3,200 a year," Rosenbluth said. "Miami was offering $5,200."

So, 40 years ago, the Rosenbluths moved south, where they have enjoyed the sunshine and weathered the hurricanes.

"We do a lot of babysitting now," laughed Rosenbluth, who retired from teaching and coaching in 1995.

Rosenbluth looks much younger than 72. He has a full head of hair, a quick smile, and a lifetime of memories. Many of those memories came from that amazing team of 1957, when a Jewish kid from The Bronx who had been cut twice from his high school team became the best collegiate basketball player in America.

LENNIE ROSENBLUTH BY THE NUMBERS

3   TIMES NAMED ALL-ACC.

10   JERSEY NUMBER (RETIRED).

10.4   CAREER REBOUNDING AVERAGE.

26.9   CAREER SCORING AVERAGE, THE HIGHEST IN UNC HISTORY.

28.0   SENIOR-SEASON SCORING AVERAGE, THE HIGHEST IN UNC HISTORY.

35   POINTS SCORED AGAINST DUKE IN ONE GAME DESPITE AN INJURY TO SHOOTING HAND (HE SHOT LEFT-HANDED INSTEAD).

45.9   CAREER FIELD-GOAL PERCENTAGE.

2,045   CAREER POINTS, THIRD IN UNC HISTORY BEHIND PHIL FORD AND SAM PERKINS.

Where Have You Gone?

PETE BRENNAN

The One-on-Two Fast Break

Pete Brennan, the leading rebounder on North Carolina's 1957 national championship team, was one of 10 children. So when he became a father, he was at least partially prepared for what lay ahead.

"I'm only half the man my father was," Brennan said with a laugh.

Ultimately, Brennan would help raise a family himself that included five children.

More importantly, growing up in a large family helped Brennan prepare for life in a large basketball family, particularly the 1957 Tar Heels. Without Brennan, the Tar Heels never would have won that national championship. As Lennie Rosenbluth would be the first to tell you, he didn't do it all by himself.

Brennan will go down in history as the player who pushed North Carolina to the famous final against Wilt Chamberlain's Kansas team in the first place. In the 1957 national semifinal, the Tar Heels trailed Michigan State, 64-62, with 11 seconds remaining in the first overtime. Michigan State's Johnny Green was at the free-throw line, shooting a one-and-one. Since there was no such thing as a three-pointer in those days, one free throw would essentially seal the game.

The Tar Heels sported a 30-0 record at the time. The Michigan State players were so confident that they would win that one of them sidled up to Tar Heel point guard Tommy Kearns before Green shot the free throw and said, somewhat cruelly: "Thirty and one!"

But Green clanked it. The 6-6, 215-pound Brennan grabbed the rebound and, instead of firing the ball upcourt to one of the Tar Heel guards, he started dribbling upcourt on the dead run.

"It was basically a one-on-two fast break," Brennan said. "I got to the foul line, and there were two Michigan State guys there. I always had great

PETE BRENNAN

1956-1958

Under Coach Frank McGuire, pictured here with Pete Brennan, the Tar Heels played "a lot of freelance basketball," according to Brennan. Now at the age of 69, Brennan can't take it easy. The former Marine is dabbling in real estate after a lengthy career in the clothing industry.

confidence in shooting a jumper from around the foul line, and I thought to myself, 'I'll take it, and I'll follow my own shot if I miss.'"

Brennan rose, shot, and scored. The game was tied at 64. Michigan State actually got off a last-second shot of its own, and it went in, but after the buzzer sounded. So, the two teams played a second overtime period and then a third, before North Carolina finally prevailed, 74-70.

That win got North Carolina into the final. Brennan had 11 points and a team-high 11 rebounds against Kansas in the 54-53 win, also accomplished in triple overtime.

The 1957 North Carolina team has long been remembered for that Final Four—which many people don't realize was actually North Carolina's second Final Four appearance. The first came in 1946, when North Carolina was still known as the "White Phantoms" and the team was led by Jim Jordan, John "Hook" Dillon, and ACC legend Horace "Bones" McKinney. That squad lost to Oklahoma A&M, 43-40, in the NCAA final. But that 1946 team is almost forgotten, while the 1957 squad still holds occasional reunions and is recognized in Chapel Hill.

When that '57 squad returned to Chapel Hill after winning the championship, thousands of people greeted them at the airport. They were chauffeured to the governor's mansion for a banquet and signed autographs for fellow students.

"It all sort of blew my mind a little bit," Brennan said.

Why did all that happen? It wasn't just the championship. It was television, too. Those two Final Four thrillers in 1957 permanently married basketball and television in North Carolina. Enthralled by the Tar Heels' undefeated record entering the Final Four, TV pioneer C.D. Chesley had put together a five-station network in North Carolina to televise the games back home. In a single week, Chesley paid a rights fee to the NCAA, found sponsors, hired broadcasters, and bought equipment.

When the Tar Heels won both games in triple OT, the folks who had TVs in the 1950s were absolutely captivated. Those telecasts set the stage for the huge TV packages the ACC can boast of today.

Brennan was a part of all that. He was another of the New Yorkers in Frank McGuire's pipeline, just as all the starters on the '57 squad were.

Basketball family aside, Brennan truly was one of 10 kids—he had six brothers and three sisters. He grew up in Brooklyn. His father, John Brennan, was a motorman for the local subway and also drove a newspaper truck. His mother, Una, raised the children.

"For 32 of his 38 years at work, my father worked two full-time jobs," Brennan said. "So school was a very important thing to him—he wanted his kids to have an education. When report card day came, he checked everybody's very closely."

The leading scorer in Brooklyn as a senior at St. Augustine's High, Brennan had a number of scholarship offers and thought seriously about Notre Dame. "Joe Quigg was already down in Chapel Hill and told me how great it was, though," Brennan said. "He really helped me make my decision."

Before Brennan, Kearns, and Quigg joined the Tar Heel varsity as sophomores (freshmen were ineligible then), Rosenbluth and his teammates struggled. In the 1954-55 season, Rosenbluth scored 25.5 a game, but the Tar Heels only went 10-11.

In 1955-56, the Brennan-Kearns-Rosenbluth-Quigg quartet first came together as the centerpiece class of Frank McGuire's reverse underground railroad. The Tar Heels improved to 18-5, but they lost to Wake Forest in the ACC tournament and thus didn't qualify for the NCAAs.

Then came 1956-57. McGuire knew he had something special, and he spent most of the Tar Heels' practices letting the players hone their skills in competitive situations.

"In practice, he just told us to scrimmage, and our scrimmages were very physical," Brennan said. "He'd stop it if he saw something he didn't like. But we never had any plays to run on offense. I mean *never*. We had two out-of-bounds plays. That was it."

Of the 32 games the Tar Heels played that year, only eight were in Chapel Hill at their Woollen Gym home. UNC learned early how to win on the road, under tough circumstances, which served the Tar Heels well when they had to beat Chamberlain's Kansas team in Kansas City.

In 1957-58, Brennan was a senior and thought the Tar Heels might be able to repeat as NCAA champions. But that team was undone by several severe injuries. It finished 19-7 but lost to Maryland in the final of the ACC tournament. Brennan was named the 1958 ACC Player of the Year, however, averaging 21.3 points and 11.7 rebounds, and was also first-team All-America. He would end up as the third-leading career rebounder per game in UNC history at 10.5, trailing only Billy Cunningham (15.4) and Doug Moe (10.6).

Drafted by the New York Knicks in the first round of the 1958 NBA draft, Brennan played in the pros for all of one season and part of another. The Knicks tried to turn him into a guard, but the experiment didn't take. Brennan barely played.

Then a different draft took hold of his life.

"The military draft was still in at the time," Brennan said, "and I was told I had to honor my obligation. So right after the second season, I joined the Marines."

After that, Brennan got into the clothing business. He had his own company for a while and also headed up a sales force out of New York for a large clothing company, selling lines like Polo, Chaps and Halston to large specialty stores. He was once contacted to see if he'd have any interest in coaching the Belmont

Abbey basketball team in North Carolina. (Al McGuire once coached there), but Brennan turned down the offer.

"That was really the last time I had anything to do with basketball," Brennan said.

Brennan does still enjoy watching the game, though. In April 2005, he traveled to St. Louis to watch the Tar Heels win the national championship. In the semifinal, he was happy to see a bit of symmetry. In another Final Four, 48 years after Brennan's own, a new Tar Heel team led by Sean May and Raymond Felton defeated another Michigan State squad in the national semifinal.

Now 69, Brennan and his wife, Jo Ellen, have five children spread out over the East Coast. Brennan lives part of the year in Jewett, New York, which is 60 miles from Albany, and is now spending more and more time in North Carolina. He recently obtained his real-estate broker's license.

"I don't know if it's being an immigrant's son or what, but I really enjoy working," Brennan said. "That's why I'm getting into real estate a little bit."

To longtime Tar Heel fans, though, the most important piece of real estate Brennan ever covered was less than 80 feet—from under his own basket to 15 feet from the Michigan State goal in 1957. For if he hadn't snared that rebound and sunk that shot, Tar Heel basketball history would have been forever altered.

PETE BRENNAN BY THE NUMBERS

10.5   CAREER REBOUNDING AVERAGE, THIRD IN UNC HISTORY BEHIND BILLY CUNNINGHAM AND DOUG MOE.

11   TOTAL OF BOTH POINTS AND REBOUNDS IN TRIPLE-OVERTIME NCAA CHAMPIONSHIP WIN OVER KANSAS IN 1957.

16.4   CAREER SCORING AVERAGE.

21.3   SCORING AVERAGE AS A SENIOR IN 1958, WHEN BRENNAN WAS ACC PLAYER OF THE YEAR AND A FIRST-TEAM ALL-AMERICAN.

35   JERSEY NUMBER (HONORED).

41.7   CAREER FIELD-GOAL PERCENTAGE.

1,332   CAREER POINTS AT UNC, WHICH STILL RANKS IN TOP 35 ALL-TIME.

Where Have You Gone?

TOMMY KEARNS

Jumping Against Wilt

He jumped center against Wilt Chamberlain—and later became Chamberlain's financial adviser. He made a movie with Sean Connery. He played in high school under Louie Carnesecca. He swished every shot he ever took in the NBA. He became a successful stockbroker on Wall Street. He still golfs occasionally with Dean Smith and Roy Williams.

Tommy Kearns, a starting guard on North Carolina's 1957 national championship team, has had a life worthy of Forrest Gump. Kearns seems to run into a lot of famous people and then get befriended by them. And when you talk to Kearns for a while, you understand why—he has a quick wit, a sharp mind, and a self-deprecating sense of humor. People naturally enjoy being around him.

It was the 5-11 Kearns whom Tar Heel coach Frank McGuire sent out to jump center against the 7-1 Chamberlain in the 1957 title game.

"It was just a ploy," Kearns said. "We weren't going to win the tip anyway. I didn't think too much of it at the time, but it became one of my defining moments. I'm sure when my obituary is written, that will be in there."

Probably so. But that fact will compete with many others in Kearns's extraordinary life, which also includes his prominent speaking role as a basketball coach in the 2000 hit movie *Finding Forrester*, which starred Connery as a reclusive novelist and Rob Brown as a high-school student who is gifted both as a writer and a basketball player.

Kearns had never acted before. But he was a friend of director Gus Van Sant's father. The movie was being filmed on location in New York—Kearns grew up in The Bronx, where his father was a policeman, and still lives in the general area. At first, Kearns was only going to be a consultant for the basketball scenes

TOMMY
KEARNS

1956-1958

Tommy Kearns (above) was a starting guard for the '57 national champs and a two-time All-ACC selection. Kearns has worked in finance for years and also had a substantial speaking part in the movie *Finding Forrester*. Here (right), Kearns and his old high school coach, Louie Carnesecca (on left), share a laugh at a charity benefit.

in the movie. But then Van Sant asked him to read for the role of Brown's high school basketball coach, and before long, Kearns had a substantial speaking part.

"It was really kind of a neat experience," Kearns said. "And I've gotten almost $70,000 in residuals from it."

When Kearns said this, it came out without a hint of braggadocio. It sounded more like wonder, as in "Can you believe this actually happened to me?"

Kearns, now 68, was good in the movie. He's been good at most things throughout his life. He picked the right woman—Betsy Wright—early in his life even though she went to the wrong school—Duke. They married in 1959.

"She's a big Carolina fan now, though," Kearns said.

He has long had a knack for managing money. After years as a Wall Street investment banker on Wall Street, Kearns still dabbles in a number of business ventures today in the health-care and biotechnology field and sits on several boards.

Even though Chamberlain was hurt by McGuire's mindgame at the beginning of the '57 championship game—which was won by North Carolina, 54-53, in triple overtime—he and Kearns ended up becoming close friends. In the early 1970s, they reconnected in New York. Chamberlain was still playing basketball, and Kearns was a well-known financial adviser. Chamberlain asked Kearns to keep him in mind if a good investment opportunity arose, and Kearns did. Many times. On one, Chamberlain (at Kearns's behest) invested some money to help purchase a bankrupt aluminum company. In three years, Kearns turned Chamberlain's $150,000 into a couple of million dollars.

"Wilt remembered that one," Kearns said, laughing, "but he always had a tendency to remind me about the ones that didn't make money, too."

The men ended up becoming close enough friends that they stayed at each others' houses many times over the years.

In 1982, the marvelous *Sports Illustrated* writer, Frank Deford, interviewed both men for a story about the 1957 Tar Heels. Chamberlain told Deford that the '57 Tar Heels were a "blessed team." As he and Kearns sat together back then, being interviewed, Chamberlain reflected about the loss against North Carolina. It had upset him for years—Chamberlain wouldn't return to the Kansas campus for 40 years after leaving it for good the following season—and he also never liked the fact that McGuire sent out Kearns for the jump ball.

Kearns, who was a good actor even in 1957, had played it up, too. Inside the jump circle, he crouched low, his muscles coiled, as if he really had a chance to spring up over Wilt the Stilt. Chamberlain won the tap, of course, but the Tar Heels had scored a psychological point.

"But that's all behind me now," said Chamberlain (who died in 1999). "I'm very lucky. You're formed by the people you know well, and I've always been fortunate, you understand, to have good people close to me ... even Kearns."

Two other interesting notes about what has to be tied for the most famous jump ball in Carolina history (along with the one Lee Dedmon lost, but that's in Chapter 16).

First, although McGuire was the one who told Kearns to go out there and do it, Kearns said jumping against Chamberlain despite his 14-inch height disadvantage was actually assistant coach Buck Freeman's idea. Freeman, a basketball junkie and the man who supplied the technical support to McGuire's psychological mastery, had seen a team send its shortest guy out on a jump ball before somewhere—"in a YMCA or something," Kearns said.

And second, Chamberlain would remember the jump ball for years, enough that he made McGuire explain the reasoning to him when McGuire became his head coach on the Philadelphia Warriors. McGuire, ironically, coached Chamberlain to his greatest individual season ever in 1961-62, when Chamberlain *averaged* 50.4 points per game and once scored an NBA-record 100.

Chamberlain scored 31,419 points in his NBA career. Kearns scored two. Kearns was a junior when the Tar Heels won the championship in 1957. In 1958, after the Tar Heels' dream of a repeat title had been snuffed out by a series of injuries, Kearns was a third-team All-American and was chosen in the fourth round of the 1958 NBA draft, by Syracuse. But Kearns didn't fit in the NBA—Syracuse cut him in favor of a future Hall of Famer named Hal Greer. Kearns got into only one real NBA game, where he played seven minutes and made the only shot he tried, a jumper from way outside. So his career field-goal percentage in the NBA remains 1.000—tied for the all-time NBA lead.

Kearns had originally been one of the New Yorkers who followed McGuire to Chapel Hill. Although Kearns's parents were concerned that his Catholicism might be a problem in the South, McGuire told them otherwise.

"The way Frank told it, we were going to save the Baptist South and convert all those heathens to Catholicism," Kearns said.

In 1959, after Kearns's basketball career ended, he started work for Merrill Lynch and got married. He served in the Army and later moved to New York, wanting to test himself in investment banking. Along the way, he and Betsy had three children and now are grandparents several times over.

Although officially retired now, Kearns is still active in the financial world. He has maintained long ties with North Carolina, serving on various financial committees and donating money. He also is a partner in the excellent Chapel Hill Sportswear shop, which has a prime location on Chapel Hill's famous Franklin Street. In 1996, the university bestowed on Kearns its "Distinguished Alumnus Award."

In 1998, the well-known writer David Halberstam developed a friendship with Kearns, one that began while they worked out alongside each other in a New York gym. Halberstam was so taken with Kearns that he wrote a long story on him in the February 7, 1999 *New York Times*. "He was smart and likable, and he clearly knew the inside of the Carolina program extremely well," Halberstam wrote.

While Kearns didn't get his hands on that tip that started the '57 championship game, he made certain that he was the last man to touch the ball as the third overtime—and the game—came to an end. He came up with a deflected pass after Kansas tried to throw a long pass to Chamberlain for one last shot, then threw it straight up in the air as the final three seconds ticked away.

"I knew intuitively that by the time the ball came down, it would be over," Kearns said.

And it was.

But Kearns's life, in many ways, never really came down to earth with that ball.

TOMMY KEARNS BY THE NUMBERS

2   TIME ALL-ACC SELECTION.

11.6   CAREER SCORING AVERAGE.

12.8   SCORING AVERAGE ON UNC'S 1957 NATIONAL CHAMPIONSHIP TEAM.

14   INCHES SHORTER THAN WILT CHAMBERLAIN, WHOM KEARNS JUMPED AGAINST ON THE OPENING TAP IN '57 NATIONAL TITLE GAME.

29   POINTS SCORED AGAINST SOUTH CAROLINA IN A 90-86 OVERTIME WIN DURING THE TITLE SEASON.

41.4   CAREER SHOOTING PERCENTAGE.

930   CAREER POINTS.

Where Have You Gone?

JOE QUIGG

Last Shot of His Life

If the final shots of your basketball life have to come at age 20, you can't go out any better than the way Joe Quigg did. Quigg hit the winning free throws with six seconds left in triple overtime against Kansas to push North Carolina ahead in the 1957 national championship game, 54-53. Then he preserved that lead by knocking a Kansas pass away from Wilt Chamberlain and to teammate Tommy Kearns on the Jayhawks' final play. Those final six seconds were like the last, brilliant burst of a shooting star before it winks out—although Quigg, then a college junior, didn't know it at the time.

Six months later, Quigg's right leg would get broken in a Tar Heel practice—rolled on from behind accidentally by two players. It would have been called clipping in football. The leg has never been quite the same since. Quigg, now 69, went on to become a successful dentist in Fayetteville, North Carolina, where he and his family have lived for the past 40 years. But he never played competitive basketball again.

"They kept me in a cast for six months," Quigg said. "Six months! That would never happen now, but that's the way it was treated back then. When the cast came off, my leg was all shriveled up. It couldn't bend."

Quigg, a junior in 1957, was a solid pro prospect when he hit the free throws to beat Kansas—a six-foot-seven center who could shoot from the outside and play good defense inside. Despite the injury, the New York Knicks took him anyway in the 1958 NBA draft and sent him back to Chapel Hill to rehabilitate his leg and serve as a volunteer assistant for the Tar Heels.

Although the leg never got better, Quigg quickly found something else to occupy his time. He had always wanted to be a dentist.

JOE QUIGG

1956-1957

Following the 1957 season, Joe Quigg (above) spent six months of his senior year in a cast after his leg was broken in practice. He is still remembered for scoring the final two points with a pair of free throws in North Carolina's 54-53 triple-overtime win over Kansas in the '57 championship game. From 1966 until his retirement in 2000, Quigg (right) was a dentist in Fayetteville, North Carolina.

"Unfortunately, I got an 'F' in the first chemistry course I ever took in Chapel Hill," Quigg said. "I took it again a couple of years later and made an 'A.' By then I had gotten a little more serious about schoolwork."

Quigg went to dental school at North Carolina, too, and finished that in 1963. Worried that he might set up a dental practice and then get drafted for Vietnam, he instead decided to go ahead and volunteer for military service.

"I wrote to my congressman and said I wanted to do that, and he wrote back saying, 'That's the first time I've ever had someone writing me wanting to get *into* the war,'" Quigg recalled.

Quigg was accepted into the U.S. Army and shipped to Stuttgart, Germany, where he practiced his dentistry on the military personnel and their dependents. When he returned to North Carolina in 1966 with his wife, Carol, he knew that many of his friends in dental school were setting up offices in the largest North Carolina cities like Charlotte and Raleigh. But the Quiggs had a connection to Fayetteville, in the eastern part of the state, and thought they would try that for a while.

The Quiggs still live in Fayetteville today. Joe Quigg was a dentist there from 1966-2000, working on the teeth of thousands of patients. He and his wife raised two children in Fayetteville, Joe and Shannan. Joe played junior varsity basketball at Carolina, where his coach was Roy Williams. The Quiggs now have five grandchildren, including nine-year-old triplets who are Shannan's.

Quigg is retired from dentistry now, but keeps busy playing golf and gardening. He's not much for vegetable gardening, but enjoys raising perennial flowers like daylilies, hostas and black-eyed Susans.

The gardening habit came about when Quigg stopped smoking. That was in 1986. Dean Smith quit two years later.

"Once, not long after that, Dean and I were at a golf tournament together and this young kid came by, threw down a cigarette butt and was about to crush it with his heel," Quigg said with a chuckle. "Dean said, 'No, don't do that. Just let me look at it for a minute.'"

Smith and Quigg both made it past their addiction, though. Quigg had grown up in Brooklyn, the oldest of Joe and Dot Quigg's three children. His father was a bank teller.

As a child, Joe Quigg was a Brooklyn Dodgers fan and was entranced by the ads that often played during the team's games for Lucky Strikes. He still remembers the jingle used to sell the cigarettes.

"Back then, just about every 11- or 12-year-old started smoking," Quigg said. "I did and kept that up until '86. By then, I was up to almost four packs a day. But I gave it up on my 50th birthday—September 22, 1986."

Quigg made a successful life for himself as a dentist and a father. But he still often remembers his days at North Carolina. His e-mail sign-on incorporates both his jersey number (41) and the year (1957) in which his Tar Heels won the national championship. Part of the reason for Quigg's fondness of that title came because the Tar Heels beat Chamberlain.

"It's important to understand what Wilt was at the time," Quigg said. "He was this creature from outer space. Nowadays, you've got everything on television. Back then the only time you'd see Wilt was on the newsreels between pictures at the theater. He was a giant from a storybook."

But the Tar Heels, helped by Quigg's 10 points and nine rebounds, beat them. In the game, Kansas opened with a box-and-one on Rosenbluth. Quigg and his teammates made them pay, opening an early 17-7 lead. They were shooting well and would rebound ferociously the entire game, outrebounding Kansas 42-28 overall. Quigg picked up his fourth foul midway through the second half. But, unlike Rosenbluth, he managed to play the rest of the game without ever picking up his fifth. By the third overtime, Quigg had played enough to feel very confident in his shot.

"I didn't always feel that way," he said. "I guess great players do all the time, but I wasn't a great player. But that night, I felt good from the beginning."

When he got the ball at the top of the key, down 53-52 with 10 seconds left in triple overtime, Quigg pump-faked and drove straight toward Chamberlain. Chamberlain lost a step on the drive, but then made up for it and angled smartly toward the basket. He blocked Quigg's shot cleanly, and that might have been it for the Tar Heels. But Chamberlain's Kansas teammate, Maurice King, had decided to try to help the big man and instead fouled Quigg.

Quigg was a 72-percent foul shooter, but he had missed the only free throw he had shot in the game. McGuire, eschewing convention, called timeout before Quigg stepped to the line.

"After Joe makes these…" McGuire started his conversation in the huddle, and whatever worries Quigg held on his shoulders dropped away. His coach *knew* he would make them. And Quigg knew it, too. He promised everyone in the huddle he wouldn't miss. Then he walked to the free-throw line.

He swished the first. He swished the second.

And then the Tar Heels made the mistake that could have cost them the 1957 national championship. McGuire wanted Chamberlain double-teamed, with Quigg in front and Danny Lotz behind him. But Lotz drifted out to the corner to guard someone else, and Quigg realized in a panic he was all alone, in front of Chamberlain. A high enough lob pass would yield a certain two points.

"Help me! Help me!" Quigg screamed to his teammates.

But it was too late. Here came the pass.

Too low.

Quigg leaped and deflected it to Kearns, who grabbed the ball and threw it exultantly in the air, and the game was over.

"We got home from the Final Four on a Sunday," Quigg said. "I had a biology exam on Tuesday, so after we got home from the airport and all the thousands that greeted us there, I just started studying."

It was a symbolic, and abrupt, changeover. Quigg's basketball life had ended. But the rest of it had just begun.

JOE QUIGG BY THE NUMBERS

0   GAMES PLAYED HIS SENIOR YEAR DUE TO LEG INJURY THAT ENDED HIS BASKETBALL CAREER.

1   PLAYER AT UNC IN LAST 50 YEARS WHOSE LAST NAME BEGAN WITH 'Q' (QUIGG IS THE ONLY ONE).

8.8   CAREER REBOUNDING AVERAGE.

11.0   CAREER SCORING AVERAGE.

34   YEARS SPENT AS A DENTIST IN FAYETTEVILLE, NORTH CAROLINA.

41.9   CAREER FIELD-GOAL PERCENTAGE.

68.4   CAREER FREE-THROW PERCENTAGE (ALTHOUGH HE MADE THE TWO THAT COUNTED MOST).

Where Have You Gone?

DONNIE WALSH

A Home in Indiana

Once upon a time, Donnie Walsh was going to be a lawyer. Following his basketball career at Chapel Hill—he's one of a handful of men who played under both coach Frank McGuire and coach Dean Smith—Walsh enrolled in law school at North Carolina. He did well academically and was one of the editors of the law review his final year. He was about to take a job with the New York firm where future President Richard Nixon worked.

But ultimately, he couldn't leave basketball. Walsh, 64, is now the CEO of the Indiana Pacers, a team he has basically run for the past 20 years. Either as general manager or CEO, Walsh has shepherded the Pacers to a stable place where they make the playoffs most every year and always contend for a title.

"All I've really got left to do is to win a championship," Walsh said.

That hasn't happened yet, and it is Walsh's grand dream. The Pacers came closest in 2000 when they made it to the NBA Finals before losing to the L.A. Lakers, four games to two.

But Walsh's career in basketball—now spanning more than 40 years—has still produced a number of exhilarating and exasperating moments. Walsh was the one who made the call in Indiana to draft Reggie Miller rather than homestate hero Steve Alford in 1987—a move that prompted a rain of boos but that ended up being the right thing to do. Walsh was also the one who had to deal with the repercussions of the Pacers-Detroit Pistons brawl with fans during a game in Michigan during the 2004-05 season. And besides being coached by both McGuire and Smith, Walsh also worked alongside both men.

"I was probably Dean's first grad assistant," Walsh recalled. "In effect, he gave me a scholarship in return for me helping to coach the freshman team while I went to law school."

DONNIE WALSH

1960-1962

Donnie Walsh (above) played for both Coach Frank McGuire and Coach Dean Smith while at UNC, and set a then-record for field goal percentage by shooting 55.9 percent as a senior. For the past 20 years, Walsh (right) has run the NBA's Indiana Pacers franchise.

Walsh would later serve as an assistant coach under McGuire for 12 seasons at South Carolina.

"Nobody had the charisma that Frank did," Walsh said. "He was this extremely magnetic man who had the ability to bring together an entire team with that charisma—and oh, by the way, he also coached a little. He was a tough man, but he conveyed that he cared about you. He liked to coach by going out on the court and letting you scrimmage, then stopping and correcting you.

"Dean? Well, Dean was one of the most brilliant guys I've ever run into. The first thing he's a really good person. He's almost the Mr. Chips of basketball. He was an extremely smart coach, and he had the most innovative ideas I'd ever heard before. He coached me first on the freshman team. And the first day he worked with me on defense, I knew I had never heard some of the stuff he talked about. And he truly regarded you as someone who was going to college, and you were just playing some basketball on the side."

Said Dean Smith: "It's pretty obvious that Donnie chose Carolina because of Frank. Donnie was a brilliant young man and a very good grad assistant. I also remember he went through about 20 Pepsis a day when he was here."

Like many of the players recruited under McGuire, Walsh was a tough New Yorker who shrank from no one. He was born and raised in a primarily Catholic community called Riverdale, in the upper Bronx. His father, Donald, was a dentist. His mother, Helen, mostly stayed home with the five kids, of which Donnie was the oldest.

During Walsh's recruitment, the Tar Heels won the 1957 national championship.

"Like so many people, I went down, visited the campus and fell in love with the place," Walsh said.

Smith coached Walsh's freshman team—and then coached Walsh again on the varsity as a senior. McGuire, who died in 1994, had Walsh for his sophomore and junior seasons.

Walsh would team with Larry Brown in the backcourt for much of his time at Carolina.

"We both brought the ball upcourt," Walsh said. "There wasn't really a point and shooting guard on our team back then."

Walsh averaged 5.6 points in the 57 games he played for the Tar Heels. The best team he played on was during his junior season of 1960-61, when McGuire's final team at North Carolina went 19-4 and won the ACC regular-season title. McGuire left after that season, however, to coach the NBA's Philadelphia Warriors. He had some problems with the North Carolina administration—particularly UNC Chancellor William Aycock—in part because of his carelessness with business receipts. The university decided to de-emphasize basketball for a while at Chapel Hill, and as part of that scheduled only 17 games in 1961-62.

That was Walsh's senior season, and the Tar Heels went 8-9. It would take 40 more years for the Tar Heels to have another losing season, when Matt Doherty's second team at UNC went 8-20. Still, Walsh was a part of Smith's first ever head-coaching victory—a 54-52 road win over Clemson on December 5, 1961.

"I like to tell people we got him win No.1," Walsh said. "But we didn't get him too many more after that."

Walsh would stay connected to Chapel Hill throughout his basketball life. After finishing law school and then becoming McGuire's assistant for 12 years, he finally decided to take the bar exam in South Carolina and passed it.

"It was an unusual combination—a coach and a lawyer," Walsh said.

His old teammate, Larry Brown, hired Walsh as his assistant with the Denver Nuggets in the late 1970s. Brown then resigned as coach in the middle of the 1978-79 season. Walsh didn't really want to be a head coach, but said he'd do it for a while. He remained the head coach for a year and a half, compiling an overall record of 60-82.

Walsh took an assistant coaching job with the Pacers in 1984. But he had a keen interest in the front office by then, one where he could draw on his experience as a coach as well as his law degree. In 1986, Walsh became the Pacers' general manager. The team was coming off a 26-56 season when Walsh took over, but under his guidance Indiana would eventually make the playoffs 13 out of 14 years. He also supervised the building of the team's 18,345-seat Conseco Fieldhouse, considered one of the finest places to play basketball in the country.

During his years in Indiana, Walsh has been able to study another hotbed of basketball, and he finds the Hoosier state to be somewhat similar to North Carolina.

"Basketball has so many deep roots in Indiana," Walsh said. "Everyone in the sport grows up in a very structured environment. Kids who are four or five years old have uniforms, coaches, the whole bit. So everyone is educated in the game and in the history of the sport. As a result, we have some great spectators."

Eventually, Walsh returned the favor he owed his old Chapel Hill backcourt mate when he hired Larry Brown to be the Pacers head coach. Brown led the Pacers from 1993 to 1997, helping them begin their steady rise toward the NBA elite. Along that path, Walsh has gained a reputation as an astute judge of talent and of people. In a 2001 poll conducted by Bloomberg News, NBA coaches voted Walsh the league's "best general manager."

Walsh would hire an even more well known Larry from the state of Indiana—Larry Bird—as well. Twice. Bird coached the Pacers from 1997 to 2000 and was named the Pacers' general manager in July 2003. Walsh is grooming Bird as his own successor.

"I plan to do this only for a couple more years," said Walsh, who along with his wife, Judy, has raised five children. "That's my timetable."

Walsh, Bird, and the entire Pacers organization had to deal with the fallout from November 19, 2004, when the Pistons and Pacers game ended because of a fight that spilled into the stands and involved fans. As a result of the fight, NBA commissioner David Stern suspended the Pacers' Ron Artest for the rest of the season. Pacer Stephen Jackson was suspended for 30 games, and Jermaine O'Neal was suspended for 25 (which an arbitrator later reduced to 15). All the suspensions were without pay.

Walsh wasn't at the game—he was in New York, attending a wedding rehearsal dinner. Then his cell phone started to ring. Over and over.

"It was a devastating event," Walsh said. "It's been one of the worst things I've ever been through, certainly, in basketball. The commissioner acted very quickly because of the negative publicity. I felt there were mitigating circumstances, because the fans in many cases were directly involved. In effect, our players were in a riot situation. Not that our players didn't do wrong—there was an awful lot of wrong that night.

"So now we are faced with this time in our history which isn't that flattering. But we will get through it. We know that the way you're judged is when things are tough, not when they are easy. We're going through all the necessary steps to make sure something like this never happens again."

DONNIE WALSH BY THE NUMBERS

5.6   WALSH'S CAREER SCORING AVERAGE.

12   SEASONS SERVED AS AN ASSISTANT UNDER FRANK MCGUIRE AT SOUTH CAROLINA.

13.4   WALSH'S SCORING AVERAGE AS A SENIOR.

55.9   FIELD-GOAL PERCENTAGE AS A SENIOR, WHICH WAS THEN A UNC RECORD.

322   WALSH'S CAREER POINTS AT UNC.

Where Have You Gone?

CHARLIE SHAFFER

Some Olympian Achievements

Charlie Shaffer was 61 years old and comfortable.

He was as embedded in the Atlanta community as the phrase "y'all." He had been a successful Atlanta trial lawyer for 37 years. He had been one of the 10 civic-minded leaders who had pulled off one of the most amazing feats in the city's history, overcoming huge odds to lure the 1996 Summer Olympics to Atlanta.

But Shaffer (rhymes with "laugher") wasn't ready to settle into retirement. And when a headhunter approached him about another job, he listened.

"After 37 years of being a trial lawyer at King & Spalding, I decided that was a gracious plenty," Shaffer said. "So I took a total right turn. And that has really invigorated me."

Now Shaffer, 63, is two years into his newest challenge. He is the president and CEO of the Marcus Institute, a remarkable place in Atlanta devoted to caring for children with learning disabilities.

The Marcus Institute (www.marcus.org) is named for Bernie Marcus, who helped start The Home Depot chain of home-improvement stores. Marcus had a longtime employee who was struggling to find the right caretakers for her son, who had a developmental disability. When he found out there was no facility in Atlanta that served a wide range of disabilities for children and adolescents, Marcus decided to build one.

Marcus, a well-known philanthropist in Georgia, has poured $70 million into the institute over the past 12 years. In that time, the institute has treated more than 20,000 kids with various problems, ranging from autism to mental retardation to pediatric feeding disorders and dozens more. It's a day-treatment facility only; there are no overnight facilities.

CHARLIE SHAFFER

1962-1964

Charlie Shaffer (above) considered himself blessed to play with three Hall of Famers as a Tar Heel: Dean Smith, Billy Cunningham and Larry Brown. Today, Shaffer (right) remains instrumental in fundraising efforts for both the University of North Carolina and the city of Atlanta, where he helped bring the 1996 Summer Olympics.

"We're the only institute like this in the Southeast, treating this broad array of disabilities under one roof," said Shaffer, who supervises 110 employees.

The kids stream in every weekday. So do the visitors who want to see up close the work being done in a facility whose motto is "Turning Disabilities into Possibilities." On the afternoon Shaffer and I met in his office, he had already hosted former First Lady Rosalynn Carter and a troupe of Secret Service agents that morning.

A former Morehead Scholar and senior-class president at North Carolina, Shaffer is no academic slouch. But his new job is a long way from business law, and his learning curve has been steep.

"One of the big challenges for me has been learning a completely different field—developmental disabilities—and I've had to learn that as I go," Shaffer said. "All lawyers work hard. But I'm working as hard if not harder here."

Age has been kind to Shaffer, who looks a bit like the late actor Gregory Peck. The energy level that allowed him to excel in two sports at UNC—and it would have been three if not for a devastating football injury—has helped him maintain a grueling work schedule. He not only helped with the Atlanta Olympic bid, but he also helped bring the 2000 Super Bowl and the 2007 Final Four to Atlanta. Shaffer also serves on a number of non-profit boards and is national co-chairman of UNC's $1.8-billion "Carolina First" fundraising campaign.

The fundraising gene came to him honestly. Shaffer's father, Charles Milton Shaffer Sr., was a UNC football standout in the 1930s who returned to Chapel Hill in 1952 to become UNC's first director of development. Charles Jr. was 10 years old at the time. From then on the university became his playground.

"I remember many a cold Saturday morning in February when my friends and I would get to Woollen Gym at 8 a.m.," Shaffer said. "A janitor would let us in, and we'd play until they kicked us out at about noon, because they had to set up the bleachers for the varsity game."

Shaffer was an excellent athlete, and by the time he was 14, Frank McGuire used to let him occasionally scrimmage with the UNC varsity. Once Shaffer was playing one-on-one with an older Tommy Kearns in an otherwise empty gym— and actually holding his own for a few moments—until Shaffer ran into a basket support on a layup and knocked out four of his own teeth.

Shaffer's best sport was football—he was a quarterback with NFL promise. Jim Tatum, UNC's football coach in the late 1950s, recruited him hard.

"Charlie really came to UNC as a football player first," recalled Dean Smith. "Tatum thought he'd be one of the great quarterbacks of all time."

But in 1960, what Shaffer still considers the most difficult point in his life occurred.

"I was playing quarterback on the freshman team, and we were playing Clemson on Fetzer Field," he said. "I went back to pass, but a defensive end came from behind me and hit me on my knee and then a defensive tackle hit me from the front. I ended up having all the ligaments in my right knee torn in two and having two knee operations. After the surgery, I developed a staph infection as well. . . . They thought they might have to amputate my leg."

Penicillin finally cured the infection, but doctors instructed Shaffer never to play football again. He was left with basketball and tennis. After a 13-month rehabilitation he joined the varsity basketball team during the second semester of his sophomore season. That was Smith's first year as head coach. Shaffer, only six-foot-three, started as a forward almost as soon as he joined the team.

The next season, in 1962-63, the Tar Heel team featured two men who would eventually make basketball's Hall of Fame as coaches (Smith and point guard Larry Brown) and one who would make it as a player (Billy Cunningham, Chapter 8). Shaffer's favorite memory of the season was UNC's 68-66 win over Kentucky in Lexington.

Recalled Shaffer: "We get in the dressing room that night and Dean says, 'When you go out there tonight and you look at those jerseys, don't see Kentucky. You just pretend it says 'Tennessee.' Psychologically, that had quite an impact on me, and I think it did on all of us."

Smith outcoached Adolph Rupp, utilizing a box-and-one on Kentucky star Cotton Nash, with Yogi Poteet frustrating Nash. Smith also employed an early version of the Four Corners, which the Tar Heels then called the "Kentucky Play." Brown ran the point. Shaffer made all five of his shots.

"I didn't reflect on it that much at the time," Shaffer said, "but I think that was the greatest game Dean ever coached."

Shaffer would go on to marry his wife, Harriet, and to law school at Chapel Hill. He and Harriet have three children and six grandchildren. He remains close to Dean Smith.

"The thing about Coach Smith is that he was such a great role model," Shaffer said, "and the principles he established for the players were carryover principles. As you moved into another field, you just absorbed those principles and took them with you. And in one way or the other, we all try to do what we can to carry them out."

CHARLIE SHAFFER BY THE NUMBERS

2   SPORTS TEAMS THAT SHAFFER CO-CAPTAINED AT UNC (BASKETBALL AND TENNIS).

5   STRAIGHT GENERATIONS OF SHAFFERS WHO HAVE ATTENDED UNC.

11.1   CAREER SCORING AVERAGE.

25   POINTS IN HIS FIRST EVER CAREER START, AGAINST CLEMSON.

Where Have You Gone?

RICHARD VINROOT

My Point—And I Do Have One

For four years, from 1991-95, Richard Vinroot was the mayor of Charlotte. The attorney and former North Carolina basketball player helped cobble together some of the deals that lured the NFL to the city. He put more police officers on the street and dramatically reorganized and reduced the size of Charlotte's city government. He did everything so well that many people urged him to run for governor of North Carolina. So he did. And he lost.

In fact, he lost the gubernatorial election three times.

So now, Vinroot, 63, has finally slowed down a little. He's still practicing business law in the same city where he's so deeply rooted, at the same Charlotte law firm where he has worked since 1969. But he's also not contemplating any more runs for public office.

"I think I've had my shot," Vinroot said as we talked in his law office. "I tried hard. I wanted to do it. I think I could have done it well. But we'll never know."

There is an air of resignation in Vinroot's tone, but also a glint in his eye. His first grandchild was born recently. He has had surgery to remove some painful bone spurs in his ankles, which has allowed him to walk without pain again. He knows more opportunities to serve will present themselves, because a man with Vinroot's connections, polish and genuine warmth is never without a full plate for long.

Vinroot's second campaign for governor, in 2000, provides a good litmus test of the loyalty of his former coach at North Carolina, Dean Smith, to all his players. Vinroot is a Republican. Smith is a Democrat. They disagree about many major hot-button issues, including the death penalty, which Smith believes should be abolished.

Nevertheless, the men are close friends. Vinroot only scored a single point in his career at North Carolina, playing so little that he only lettered in one of his

31

UNC Athletic Communications

RICHARD VINROOT

1962

Although he was class president at Chapel Hill during his junior and senior years, Richard Vinroot (above) had a hard time earning playing time on Coach Smith's first UNC squad in 1961-62. His teammates included Larry Brown, Charlie Shaffer, and Donnie Walsh. Since 1969, Vinroot (right) has worked as a business lawyer for the same law firm in Charlotte. He was also the mayor of Charlotte for four years and ran unsuccessfully for governor of North Carolina.

two years on the varsity. But when Vinroot volunteered to go to Vietnam in 1966—he had originally been rejected by the draft board because he was too tall at six-foot-seven—Smith thought of him all the time.

"When I was in Vietnam, I'd get a letter a week from my Mom, my wife, and Coach Smith," Vinroot said. "They were my regular correspondents. And here's me, a guy who contributed zilch to the program. This coach is treating me as if I was some very special graduate."

More than 30 years later, Vinroot asked Smith to film a TV ad supporting his run for governor. Smith agreed. Why?

"We do disagree politically," Smith said in our interview for this book. "But I owe Richard. I owe all these guys. I said in the ad I would certainly support him as a person. I was careful not to say directly, 'Vote for Richard,' but I definitely bragged on him."

Smith caught all sorts of flak for the ad. Vinroot won the Republican nomination in 2000, but then lost to Democrat Mike Easley. In 2004, Vinroot ran again. This time, though, he finished second by an eyelash in the Republican primary to Patrick Ballantine. With the chance to call for a two-candidate runoff—the original field had included six Republicans—Vinroot instead bowed out entirely and allowed Ballantine the nomination and an extra month to campaign as the Republican choice. (Ballantine still lost to Easley.)

For that third and final run at governor in 2004, Vinroot decided not to ask Smith for an encore TV ad performance. He didn't want his old coach to open himself up to any political potshots. Vinroot also playfully noted that Smith is still trying to change Vinroot's mind about issues like abortion and the death penalty.

"Coach Smith doesn't give up," Vinroot said. "He periodically will send me columns he's clipped out on these subjects, hoping I'll see the error of my ways."

As a boy, Vinroot's father came to America from Sweden. The family's Swedish surname could have been easily Anglicized to "Peterson." But the family had been very poor in Sweden. Like so many immigrants, they were searching for a new start in a better place.

Said Vinroot: "The wealthiest family in southern Sweden at that time were the Winroths. And the way a Swede pronounces that is 'Vinroot.' So my grandfather and mother got here and they said, 'This is America, we're going to be Vinroots.'"

Vinroot's father started a construction company from scratch in Charlotte. Richard Vinroot was the oldest of the family's three children and a high achiever almost from the moment he left the womb. He was an Eagle Scout. He was a high-school football and basketball star at East Mecklenburg. He won a Morehead Scholarship to UNC. He was both junior- and senior-class president at Chapel Hill—his roommate and teammate, Larry Brown, was his vice president for both years.

In Charlotte, after coming home from Vietnam, Vinroot was a tireless civic leader. He taught Sunday School, led a Boy Scout troop in the inner city, volunteered at the YMCA and helped set up a charter school for poor children. He served eight years on Charlotte's City Council before his two two-year terms as mayor, which meant he won six local elections in a row.

Until he reached his late 50s and lost a few statewide elections, about the only thing Vinroot didn't succeed at was earning playing time under Smith.

"I was one of the reasons Dean Smith was later hung in effigy," Vinroot said, laughing.

Vinroot met his wife, the former Judy Allen, while at Chapel Hill. They would later raise three children of their own. Judy now teaches at a Charlotte community college.

Then, Judy was a cheerleader at UNC. Richard was a benchwarmer.

"When I went into the game, I was clearly a human victory cigar," Vinroot said. "I played so little that after a game I was dry and clean. There was no need for me to shower. But Judy had worked so hard in the game that she would have to go and shower and I would wait for her after the game, not the reverse."

Vinroot came close to being held scoreless throughout his career. But on January 6, 1961, in Charlotte, he played for the Tar Heels against Notre Dame and was fouled on a shot. He missed his first free throw and made his second.

But he did make his point—as he would in many elections both won and lost over the ensuing years. His one regret is that he didn't become governor of North Carolina.

"I was persistent," Vinroot said, "but I didn't seem to have it in the end. I sure tried. I don't know what it was. Maybe I'm just not electable. But there are other ways to serve, and I will continue to pray about that. I still teach my Sunday School class [at Myers Park Presbyterian] for high school kids. I'll be a good grandfather. And I hope other avenues will open for me."

RICHARD VINROOT BY THE NUMBERS

1   POINT SCORED AT UNC.

3   PEOPLE WHO WROTE VINROOT MOST FREQUENTLY WHILE HE SERVED IN VIETNAM (HIS MOTHER, HIS WIFE AND DEAN SMITH).

4   YEARS SERVED AS CHARLOTTE'S MAYOR.

8   YEARS SERVED ON CHARLOTTE'S CITY COUNCIL.

9   GAMES PLAYED AT UNC.

36   CONSECUTIVE YEARS AT SAME CHARLOTTE LAW FIRM.

Where Have You Gone?

BILLY
CUNNINGHAM

The Kangaroo Kid Grows Up

He's not a kid anymore. Billy Cunningham still can play a mean game of squash, and he still has some of that red hair left. But he's 62 years old now, not 22. He lives in the Philadelphia area, doing some charitable work and long retired from his NBA career as player, TV announcer, coach and part-owner. He hasn't jumped as high as a kangaroo in a long time.

Nevertheless, Cunningham's name remains one of those etched in gold in the memories of Carolina basketball fans. He was Dean Smith's first truly great player—an eventual Basketball Hall of Famer whose leaping ability was only one of his attributes. Cunningham also possesses an innate sense of decency and a knack for making good decisions quickly. That served him very well in the NBA, when he won NBA championships in his adopted hometown of Philadelphia both as a player (1967) and coach (1983).

It also served him well when he spearheaded the move to break up the nasty party as Dean Smith was getting hung in effigy on the Chapel Hill campus in January 1965. The Tar Heels were 6-6 at the time and on a three-game losing streak when their team bus pulled up in front of Woollen Gym on the UNC campus after their latest loss. A dummy that was obviously Smith—its nose was very long—had been hung by some students with a homemade noose.

"We had just lost to Wake Forest," recalled Cunningham in our interview for this book. "You have to understand, we were not very good. We had been on probation and couldn't recruit much outside the state. There was segregation. We had no black players. We had two or three walk-ons among our top seven or eight players.

"When the bus pulled up, I think we were mainly disappointed in ourselves. If anything, we thought we had let Coach Smith down [in the 22-point Wake

BILLY CUNNINGHAM

1963-1965

Billy Cunningham (above) was "extremely important to our program in so many ways," said Dean Smith. Cunningham was a two-time All-American at UNC who once scored 48 points and grabbed 25 rebounds in the same collegiate game. Cunningham went on to a productive career as a player and then coach in the NBA, winning two championships. Here (right), Cunningham appears at a recent golf tournament in the Charlotte area.

Forest loss]. Someone had to explain to us what being hung in effigy was all about, and once they did we were upset that people would do that and blame him."

Cunningham, then a college senior, got off the bus, grabbed the effigy and ripped it down. A teammate, Billy Galantai, helped him. Smith has said many times since that he's just glad the students hung a dummy instead of the real thing. The incident has become something the coach can joke about now, for we all know how things turned out for him at Carolina. But at the time, no one knew how it would turn out for Smith and the Tar Heels.

Cunningham's spontaneous gesture was one of those galvanizing moments that has united Carolina basketball over the decades. We stick together, that gesture said, no matter what others think of us.

Noted Smith in our interview for this book: "And Billy played very well in our next game against Duke, too."

Indeed, Carolina pulled an upset over Duke three days later.

Although Cunningham played all his college basketball under Smith, he came to Carolina because of Frank McGuire. Cunningham was a schoolboy star in Brooklyn. On his fifth birthday he had received a basketball from his father, and it was rarely out of his hands after that. His father was an assistant chief of the New York Fire Department.

"And after he put all his kids through school," Cunningham said proudly, "Dad went back to school himself at age 57."

As for recruiting, the Cunningham family wasn't a very hard sell.

"The key was Frank," Cunningham said. "Frank was wired in New York City. His sister lived right around the block from me. To this day, one of my sister's best friends is Frank McGuire's niece."

Smith, who was McGuire's top assistant when Cunningham was being recruited in 1961, generally stayed behind to run practice while McGuire went on the road. But Smith did go on a recruiting visit to Cunningham's home with McGuire.

"It sounded pretty good," Smith said. "It seemed like McGuire and Billy's father were not only good friends, but everybody in New York was also a mutual friend of theirs."

Cunningham said his father told him later that he either needed to go to a Catholic school or down to Chapel Hill to play for "Uncle Frank." Billy C. chose Carolina. But by the time Cunningham arrived in the fall of 1961, McGuire was gone in a dispute with the chancellor and had left to coach the NBA's Philadelphia Warriors.

Cunningham stayed anyway and had a marvelous three years. Once he became eligible for the varsity as a sophomore, he quickly established himself as Smith's best player. No one in Carolina history has ever rebounded as well as

Cunningham—his stunning average of 15.4 rebounds per game is nearly five higher than the next highest UNC career average (Doug Moe at 10.6).

As a sophomore during the 1962-1963 season, Cunnningham made a shot from almost halfcourt to send a game against Notre Dame into overtime. The Tar Heels would eventually win it. Bobby Lewis watched that game on TV and later would say that was one of the reasons he came to Carolina.

That was also the season that Cunningham and his teammates helped get Smith his first big win: a 68-66 upset of Kentucky on December 17, 1962. While Cunningham's teammate Charlie Shaffer mostly remembers telling Smith after the game it was the greatest game anyone has ever coached, Cunningham remembers a conversation he had with Kentucky coach Adolph Rupp after the game.

"We just had one of those great nights where everyone contributed," Cunningham said.

"After the game, I happened to walk by Rupp and said, 'Coach, good luck the rest of the season!' He looked right at me and growled, 'Boy, you were lucky!'"

Two years later, Cunningham would lead another North Carolina squad that would whip Kentucky, 82-67, in Charlotte.

"We just kicked their butt that time," Cunningham remembered.

This time Rupp had a different take on the game. He went to visit Cunningham in the Tar Heel locker room.

"Boy," Rupp said, "you want to come play in my all-star game?"

Cunningham got to play in a lot of all-star games. Although his Tar Heel teams never did win the conference, his statistics from those years are somewhat mind-boggling. In one game against Tulane, Cunningham had 48 points and 25 rebounds. Against Maryland once, he had 40 points and 28 boards. He had 27 points and 23 rebounds in one win over Virginia.

"He was a 6-4 post man for us," said Smith, who still plays golf with Cunningham several times a year, "and then he grew two inches while he was here."

Cunningham was a No. 1 draft choice of the Philadelphia 76ers in 1965, beginning what would be a 40-year relationship with that city that is still going strong.

"My NBA career was interesting," Cunningham said. "Even though I had a two-year guaranteed contract, I really didn't know if I was going to make it. It was like going up a ladder. I made it, then I wanted to play a lot, then I wanted to start, and then I wanted to play in an all-star game and try to make All-Pro."

He did all of that, of course. Cunningham averaged 20.8 points per game in his NBA career and played on a great team in 1966-67 that went 68-13 in the regular season and won the NBA championship behind Wilt Chamberlain, Hal Greer, Chet Walker, and Cunningham.

After seven years with the 76ers, Cunningham jumped ship to the ABA's Carolina Cougars for two seasons.

"That move was purely for money," Cunningham said. "The Cougars were going to pay me somewhere around $300,000 a year, and they wouldn't even pay me $90,000 in Philly."

Cunningham was the ABA's MVP in 1972-73—and said he had never been more tired in his life. The Cougars split their home games between Greensboro, Charlotte, and Raleigh.

"So for most home games you had to get in your car and drive for a couple of hours," Cunningham said.

Cunningham returned to Philadelphia for his final two seasons, ending his playing career in 1976. He started doing some TV broadcasting. But then, despite the fact that he had no coaching experience, the 76ers decided to hire him as their head coach in late 1977. Drawing on his days at UNC from the beginning, Cunningham was a huge success. His all-time winning percentage was .698 from 1977-85, when he gave up coaching entirely.

The 76ers made it to the NBA Finals three times under Cunningham's tutelage and won it all in 1983 on a team that included Moses Malone, Julius Erving, and North Carolina product Bobby Jones. In 1985, though, Cunningham stepped down. He was only in his early 40s and could have conceivably coached for another 20-25 years.

"But my children [the Cunninghams have two daughters, Heather and Stephanie] were getting toward being teenagers," Cunningham said. "As parents, we didn't want to look back and have problems. They were our priority. Plus I had become very tired of the travel. Everybody thought I would come back and coach again at some point, but I never have."

Cunningham did come back to basketball, however, first as a TV announcer and then as an NBA part-owner. He and a friend he had known since kindergarten, Lewis Schaffel, started working toward getting an NBA expansion franchise in Miami.

"We worked our tails off for two years—getting a lease, selling season tickets and raising money," Cunningham said. "To make it happen was very fulfilling."

In 1994, Cunningham and Schaffel—who had invested their own money heavily into the franchise eventually known as the Miami Heat—sold their shares at a hefty profit.

"It just wasn't fun anymore," Cunningham said. "I felt like it was time to move on."

Since then, Cunningham has made himself busy in various charity endeavors, including a learning center for children in Philadelphia and raising money for a statue of former teammate Wilt Chamberlain.

For more than 20 years, Cunningham also owned a small pub in Philadelphia called "Billy Cunningham's Court." It was recently sold, however, to a group of former lacrosse players. Cunningham also finds a little time for golf—and a lot for his grandchildren.

"I've been very fortunate," Cunningham said. "My life has been a lot of fun."

BILLY CUNNINGHAM BY THE NUMBERS

2   TIMES ALL-AMERICAN AT UNC.

2   NBA CHAMPIONSHIPS, ONE AS A PLAYER (1967) AND ONE AS A COACH (1983).

15.4   REBOUNDING AVERAGE PER GAME AT UNC, A RECORD THAT LIKELY WILL NEVER BE SURPASSED.

20.8   CAREER SCORING AVERAGE IN NBA.

24.8   CAREER SCORING AVERAGE AT UNC.

48, 25   POINTS, REBOUNDS IN A SINGLE GAME AGAINST TULANE.

61   GAMES WITH 10 OR MORE REBOUNDS AT UNC.

69.8   WINNING PERCENTAGE AS AN NBA COACH.

Where Have You Gone?

BILL HARRISON

From Benchwarmer to CEO

There are dozens of North Carolina basketball lettermen who will always be remembered for their dunks, their game-winning jumpers and highlight reel plays. But Bill Harrison isn't one of them. In fact, if you only watch ESPN and have never tuned into CNBC, you probably don't have a clue who Bill Harrison is.

Harrison got one of the first scholarships coach Dean Smith ever awarded, then scored exactly one basket in his entire North Carolina basketball career. The 6-4 Rocky Mount, N.C., native only played basketball for two seasons—one on the freshman team in 1962-63 and then one as a varsity benchwarmer in 1963-64.

Following his sophomore season, Harrison walked into Dean Smith's office and gave up his scholarship to concentrate on his academics. It was a wise move. Harrison ultimately ascended to chairman and CEO of JPMorgan Chase, the second largest bank in the world. The soft-spoken, self-deprecating Southerner is one of the most powerful businessmen in the universe and leader of a company that employs 160,000 people.

With that sort of power comes plenty of connections. Erskine Bowles, who served as President Clinton's chief of staff, is one of Harrison's best friends. When Dean Smith was invited to a state dinner at the White House in 1998, the coach was gratified to find that Harrison was there as well. Harrison still maintains a deep connection with his alma mater, his former teammates, and with Coach Smith, whom Harrison has felt grateful to for years for some of the small kindnesses Smith showed to Harrison long before Harrison became a phenomenally successful banker.

UNC Athletic Communications

BILL
HARRISON

1964

Bill Harrison (above) scored just two points during his brief North Carolina career, quitting basketball after his sophomore season to focus on his academics. The move paid off: Harrison is now one of the world's most powerful businessmen, serving as chairman and CEO of JPMorgan. In the spring of 2005, Harrison invited a prestigious trio (right) to accompany him to play Augusta National, where he is a member. From left: Erskine Bowles (who was once President Clinton's Chief of Staff), Harrison, Dean Smith, and Roy Williams.

Courtesy of Bill Harrison

"All I've done all these years is ride the coattails of Carolina basketball," Harrison laughed.

Well, not quite.

But Harrison's story of Tar Heel basketball is an interesting one. He played in fewer games for North Carolina than anyone else included in this book (although he may ultimately be the richest of them all). He literally quit the team. Yet Smith has embraced Harrison just as he has all of his other players.

Harrison got his scholarship before entering Chapel Hill in 1962. Only a few months before, Frank McGuire had left as the Tar Heels' head coach to coach the NBA's Philadelphia Warriors, and Dean Smith had been promoted. McGuire had committed some NCAA violations (mostly due to his carelessness with business receipts) and was not on good terms with UNC Chancellor William Aycock. Aycock had hired Smith, McGuire's young assistant, and also decided to temporarily de-emphasize basketball at Chapel Hill. Among the Tar Heels' self-imposed punishments: only 17 games in 1961-62 and only two recruits allowed outside of the region.

"For me, all that was probably a good thing," Harrison said. "They could only give two out-of-state scholarships out of six. So out of the four in-state scholarships available, I got one. I probably wouldn't have gotten one otherwise."

Harrison had grown up in Rocky Mount, where his grandfather was a banker and his father a businessman who also lettered in basketball for the Tar Heels in the 1930s. Harrison took a post-graduate year at Virginia Episcopal school in Lynchburg, Virginia, before enrolling at Chapel Hill.

After playing a good deal on the freshman team, Harrison lettered but was little more than a practice player as a sophomore on a team that included Billy Cunningham. Concerned about how difficult it was to balance his academics, basketball, and being an active member of a fraternity, Harrison decided basketball should be the thing to go.

"I talked to my Dad first, because he was a very important guy in my life and a Carolina letterman, and I thought I might be letting him down," Harrison recalled. "But he said, 'I'll totally support you.' So then I went to see Coach Smith in the spring. I was just dreading it. Basically, I was going in there to quit, and you never feel good about that."

Smith, at the time, was a young coach of 33. But he let Harrison off gracefully. Still, Harrrison wasn't quite sure everything was all right.

"In most programs, the day I walked out of that office would have been the day that ended any connection I had to the program," Harrison said. "And deep down, I was concerned that I'd let Coach Smith and the program down."

It was months before Harrison saw Smith again. Then Harrison took a date to The Pines restaurant in Chapel Hill (the same restaurant Smith had already helped integrate as an assistant coach when he brought a young black man from his church as his guest to eat dinner there).

Smith came up to Harrison's table and made sure he felt welcome, chatting for a long time with him. Not long afterwards, the coach left and waved goodbye. When Harrison and his date asked for their check a few minutes later, the waiter had a message.

"Coach Smith has already taken care of it," the waiter said.

"That sent me a signal that everything was okay," Harrison recalled. "All of a sudden, I knew he was okay with what I did. And of course, he stayed in touch like he does with everybody, long before I became a CEO."

Harrison graduated from Carolina in 1966. He was in the Coast Guard reserve for six months and then joined Chemical Bank. He moved to New York in 1967, figuring he would come home to the South at some point.

"But I've never left," Harrison said. "It's been more than 38 years now. I love going to work and I love New York City. The vibrancy. The business opportunities. It's just fun being in the middle of the greatest city in the world."

Smith always left Harrison and the other Carolina lettermen in the New York area several tickets at Madison Square Garden whenever the Tar Heels played there. He sends Harrison a media guide of the current team each season, just like he does for every letterman.

"We have kept in touch for a long time," Smith said in our interview for this book before proceeding to rattle off all sorts of details about Harrison's life. "He's done pretty well, hasn't he?"

For years, Harrison hoped to find a way to repay a bit of Smith's kindness. He found one after getting invited to join the exclusive membership at Augusta National, where The Masters golf tournament is held every April. Harrison has taken Smith to golf there a couple of times now, each time with some other friend like Roy Williams, Bowles, and Tommy Kearns.

The two also intersected in 1998 at a state dinner for South Korean president Kim Dae Jung. Recalled Smith: "I was so relieved to walk into the room and see Bill Harrison. I was afraid I wasn't going to know another person."

Said Harrison: "We saw each other at the reception and after dinner was over the president [Bill Clinton] invited Erskine and Coach Smith and I and our wives up to his study and we sat up and talked for two or three hours. It was fantastic."

Then came the not-so-fantastic part. Although Smith stayed the night in the White House, the Harrisons needed to get back to New York. They were supposed to have a driver waiting for them outside the White House, but they also were supposed to have come back to the car around 10 p.m. Instead, because of Clinton's invitation, the Harrisons had been delayed until almost 1 a.m. By the time they got onto the street and the White House doors had clanged shut behind them, it took them only a few moments to realize the car had left. They were stranded on the street in a tuxedo and long gown.

"And when you're outside the White House, you are out," Harrison said. "There was no way to get back in there."

Said Harrison to his wife, Anne: "Ten minutes ago we were with the president. Now we're about to get mugged."

Fortunately, a cab passed by before too long and whisked the Harrisons away.

Harrison, his wife and their two young daughters now live in Greenwich, Connecticut. Harrison didn't get married until age 42 and didn't have children until 47. His daughters are both excellent squash players.

"I wanted to get them involved in sports as early as I could," Harrison said.

In July 2006, Harrison will be 62 years old. At that time, his current contract based on the bank's latest merger calls for him to give up the CEO title of JPMorgan Chase. His duties at the bank will diminish, and he will have more free time, although he will remain very involved in bank business.

Harrison teaches a leadership class at the bank and has long drawn on the example Smith has set.

"I tell our people a lot that it's not necessarily the best talent that wins, it's the team that has the best culture," Harrison said. "What do we believe in? How do we treat each other? How do we work together? The right values and the right beliefs will win. The Detroit Pistons could never have beaten the L.A. Lakers on pure talent [in the 2004 NBA Finals], but they had a better team and a better coach.

"The greatest satisfaction I get is building a team and creating value for both employees and shareholders," Harrison continued. "When that starts happening, it's very satisfying. When it doesn't happen, it's like losing."

But for someone who only scored a single basket in his North Carolina career, Harrison ended up far from a loser.

"When you get to be a CEO at a big bank, the press becomes interested in every part of your life," Harrison said. "They love to hear that I played basketball for Dean Smith and, if you don't watch it, they'll imply I was some sort of star down there. I've always tried to defuse that, but I've still gotten more of a halo effect than I ever deserved. I'll say it once more—all I've really done is just ride the coattails of that wonderful brand that Coach Smith has created."

BILL HARRISON BY THE NUMBERS

1   SEASON ON THE UNC VARSITY.

2   TOTAL POINTS IN UNC CAREER.

50.0   CAREER FIELD-GOAL PERCENTAGE (1 FOR 2).

160,000 EMPLOYEES AT THE BANK WHERE HARRISON IS CEO.

Where Have You Gone?

LARRY MILLER

"I Just Played the Game"

Even now, 40 years after Larry Miller first arrived on the Chapel Hill campus, his name alone sends shivers of recognition through long-time Tar Heel fans. In the late 1960s at North Carolina, Miller was a basketball demi-god. His successful recruitment marked the first time Dean Smith had ever gone head to head against Duke for a big-time player—and won.

Miller is the only two-time ACC Player of the Year in UNC history. Even without a three-point line and with no freshman eligibility, Miller still ranks sixth all-time in scoring at UNC (trailing only Phil Ford, Sam Perkins, Lennie Rosenbluth, Al Wood and Charlie Scott). He was incredibly consistent and still holds the North Carolina record for consecutive games scoring in double figures at 64.

So what happened to him after his days as a Tar Heel ended? Fans ask that question about the mysterious Miller as much as any other Tar Heel in history. He played six years in the ABA, once scoring 67 points in a single game. He could have been an actor at one point—his rugged handsomeness had been noticed by Hollywood—but he walked away from a seven-year contract.

Miller never married or had children. Now 59 years old and semi-retired, he splits his time between Virginia Beach and Pennsylvania, dabbling on eBay and also in real estate. He loves libraries and is an avid reader.

Miller was a landmark for both Smith and the basketball program. A 6-4, 215-pound lefty, Miller was built like one of the Mack trucks that his father worked on as a mechanic for 43 years in Pennsylvania. Every school in the country wanted Miller when he was coming out of Catasauqua, Pennsylvania. No wonder—he was also a great leaper who could put both elbows on the rim while dunking the ball.

LARRY MILLER

1966-1968

Larry Miller was named ACC Player of the Year twice—the only Tar Heel to earn that distinction. According to Miller, in high school, wearing a pair of Chuck Taylors and playing on a concrete floor, he could put both elbows on the rim when he dunked. Today, Miller, an avid reader, dabbles in real estate and on eBay, and splits his time between Virginia and Pennsylvania.

"I got a lot of illegal offers," he said in our interview for this book. "I could have had summer jobs making more money than my father made in an entire year. It was tempting to hear it, but there was no way I would accept anything. I was setting up bowling pins when I was 10 years old. I had a work ethic, instilled by my family. The people who offered me illegal stuff—their programs either were in trouble or got in trouble pretty fast after that."

He still remembers his days at North Carolina fondly, especially the ACC tournaments.

"It's hard to understand now," Miller said. "But at that time, the ACC tournament was bigger than a presidential election. It was *bigger* than the Final Four. It was the *deal*. You had to win three straight games to get into the NCAAs, or else you were out. You talk about pressure! I wouldn't sleep for three days during the tournament. My stomach would kill me, I wanted to do well so badly."

And he almost always did.

"He was built like a football linebacker," said Woody Durham, the longtime radio voice of the Tar Heels. "In his prime, he could definitely play today."

Said Dean Smith: "He was really an important player for us. Bobby Lewis helped recruit him, and my assistant Ken Rosemond had a really good relationship with him. What a great competitor he was. He could drive, he had an outside shot, and he was a really strong rebounder for his size."

In Miller's three years, the Tar Heels won all but one of their ACC tournament games, losing in Miller's sophomore year by a single point to Duke. During Miller's junior and senior seasons, the Tar Heels made the Final Four— the first two appearances (out of 11) for Dean Smith-coached Carolina teams.

"I didn't really have any favorite moves," said Miller, who averaged 21.8 points a game during his career. "I just played the game. I was probably one of the best drivers there ever was, going to the basket. I had a mid-range jump shot, and I was very strong for the time, so I got a lot of baskets on rebounds. I brought the ball up for us some in pressure situations. I just had a nose for the ball. If you look at the way Dwyane Wade plays now for the Miami Heat—that's almost a mirror image of my game."

Miller was truly torn between North Carolina and Duke as a high school senior. He didn't announce where he was going until his high school graduation. He had once thought of going to Michigan, too. But during his recruiting visit to Ann Arbor in 1963, President John F. Kennedy was assassinated. Miller couldn't get that out of his mind from then on whenever he thought of Michigan.

"I still didn't really know that morning of my graduation where I was going to go," Miller said. But he liked Smith and his staff, and he always remembered the recruiting visit he took to Chapel Hill where Billy Cunningham had taken such an interest in him.

"I think the key to the whole thing was Larry Miller," recalled Cunningham. "Bobby Lewis was a great recruit for Dean, too. But when Miller came, that just turned the whole place around."

Miller said the Final Fours he played in during 1967 and '68 for North Carolina were actually anticlimactic after the ACC tournaments. The Tar Heels lost to Dayton in the national semifinals in '67 and then to UCLA (and the dominant Lew Alcindor) in the national final in 1968.

"You put so much energy into winning the ACC tournament back then," Miller said, "that by the time you got to Final Four, it really wasn't as big of a deal."

In 1968, Miller made first-team All-America, joining one of the most star-studded All-America casts there ever will be. Pete Maravich, Wes Unseld, Elvin Hayes, and Alcindor (later Kareem Abdul-Jabbar) filled out the consensus first-team squad. Bob Lanier, Jo Jo White, and Calvin Murphy were relegated to the second team.

That was also the year that after the Tar Heels returned from the 23-point loss to UCLA in the national final, North Carolina boosters gave Dean Smith a Carolina blue Cadillac convertible.

"I'm not the Cadillac type," Smith said. But he added: "I accept the gift because I am certain you are really expressing appreciation for the fine play of our team."

Miller's pro career was spent entirely in the ABA, a zany pro league with the stability of a sandcastle. In six full ABA seasons, Miller averaged 13.6 points per game and played for nine different coaches. One of the coaches was Wilt Chamberlain, who supervised Miller's San Diego Conquistadors in 1973-74.

"Wilt didn't show up for many of our practices," Miller recalled. "And when he came to the games, I didn't get to play at all. I guess he didn't like me."

When Miller played, though, he always could score. Once in 1972, while playing for the ABA's Carolina Cougars, he poured in 67 points on "Richard Petty Night" in Greensboro Coliseum.

Said Petty, the famous race car driver, after the game to Miller: "It was supposed to be my night, but it turned into yours."

Although Miller averaged 18.4 points for the Cougars in 1971-72, they wouldn't give him a raise from $45,000 to $60,000 a season as he requested. He had to move to the San Diego franchise to get it. While in California, he got interested in acting.

"I studied at Universal Studios for about two years," Miller said. "I went through all these classes, and then I did a tryout for the studio brass. They offered me a seven-year contract, where you make a studio wage and they put you in different shows. But I was still playing basketball, and I didn't think I wanted to stop. So I just walked away from it."

His basketball career lasted until 1974. Then, tired of the ABA's uncertain future, Miller left basketball entirely at the relatively young age of 28. From then on, Miller mostly sold real estate in Virginia Beach. For years, he kept in shape by running. He has completed three marathons in his lifetime.

In 1985, nearly 20 years after he finished his basketball career at Chapel Hill, Miller earned his degree in business administration.

"I was one of the few Dean ever had who didn't graduate," Miller said, laughing. "That truly bothered me. I knew I was hurting his graduation percentage. So I went back and took the one class I needed, commuting from Virginia Beach down to Chapel Hill for a Tuesday/Thursday class every week. They treated me just like a scholarship athlete—I had to report to Coach [Bill] Guthridge on my progress. I froze on one test, aced the final and ended up with a B-plus. It was fun. Even now, I'm really fascinated by learning."

Since his mother's death, Miller has spent more time in Pennsylvania, trying to tie up loose ends in his hometown and doing some charity work for the local library in Catasauqua.

"I've enjoyed becoming more literate on the computer in the past few years," Miller said. "I'm never going to totally retire, but it is nice to take things easy. I'm really not sure what I'm going to do for the rest of my life."

LARRY MILLER BY THE NUMBERS

1	SHOT MISSED (OUT OF 14) IN A 32-POINT PERFORMANCE AGAINST DUKE IN THE '67 ACC TOURNAMENT FINAL.
9	PLAYERS WHO HAVE EVER BEEN NAMED ACC PLAYER OF THE YEAR TWICE. MILLER IS THE ONLY ONE OF THOSE NINE WHO CAME FROM UNC.
9.2	CAREER REBOUNDING AVERAGE.
21.8	CAREER SCORING AVERAGE.
64	SCHOOL-RECORD NUMBER OF GAMES IN A ROW THAT MILLER SCORED IN DOUBLE FIGURES.
67	POINTS SCORED IN AN ABA GAME FOR THE CAROLINA COUGARS.
1,982	POINTS SCORED AT UNC (SIXTH IN SCHOOL HISTORY).

BILL BUNTING

Steady As He Goes

Bill Bunting still wonders about it occasionally. What if North Carolina players in the 1960s had the sort of strength and conditioning training that the Tar Heel teams enjoy today?

"If I could have picked up 20 good pounds, who knows where that would have led me?" Bunting asked as we sat at a bookstore/café in Raleigh.

As it was, Bunting still had a fine career at North Carolina. He started on three consecutive UNC Final Four teams as a skinny, 6-9 power forward who never weighed more than 200 pounds in college. But he could run the floor and had an accurate mid-range jumper.

Bunting remains both thin and active today. He works in Raleigh as a housing officer for the North Carolina Housing Finance Agency. Bunting's job is basically to help create affordable housing opportunities for families who are struggling to buy a house through various state programs and partnerships. He has literally helped thousands of first-time homeowners in N.C. during his 11 years in the job.

Bunting is a rarity among North Carolina players of the 1950s and '60s because of his deep roots to the state. Most players from that generation either came from somewhere else—usually New York or Pennsylvania—or eventually settled somewhere else. Or both. But not Bunting. He grew up in eastern North Carolina, so his deep Southern accent is well-earned. He went to school in-state and has worked in-state nearly his entire adult life, buying UNC basketball season tickets every year. At age 58, he still has a full head of brown hair and wears glasses that give him a professorial look.

UNC Athletic Communications

BILL BUNTING

1967-1969

At 6-9 and 200 pounds (or less), Bill Bunting (above) was a lanky power forward who started for three straight Final Four teams. He averaged 18 points as a senior, setting a then-UNC record for field goal accuracy at 59.8 percent. Today, Bunting (right) works in Raleigh as a housing officer for the North Carolina Housing Finance Agency.

Bunting's father was E.H. Bunting. He was 6-4 and 280 pounds. Everyone called him "Speed" as a joke because E.H. was so slow. Speed ran a lumber company in New Bern, N.C., where he and his wife, Julia, raised their family.

E.H. Bunting loved sports, too. He had graduated from Duke University way back when it was still known as "Trinity."

Bunting was a Duke fan as a kid. But he had an older brother, Harry, who went to UNC. That helped even the stakes when Bunting started getting recruited by both schools. Bunting ultimately picked UNC and became part of the well-known Class of 1969 that also included Dick Grubar, Franklin "Rusty" Clark, Jim Bostick, Joe Brown, and Gerald Tuttle. That class won every ACC tournament from 1967-69 and participated in three consecutive Final Fours.

Said former North Carolina coach Bill Guthridge: "Bill Bunting was a very quiet guy who stayed within himself and became a heck of a player by the time he was through. I think the best game he ever had for us was in 1968, when we beat Ohio State in the Final Four. In a very big game, he was just outstanding."

As a sophomore and junior, Bunting averaged right around eight points and six rebounds per game. But then he decided to stay at Chapel Hill before his senior year, working out on his own with weights and running a lot. Gradually, he became much better. In 1968-69, Bunting was second on the team in both scoring (18.0) and rebounding (7.7) and became a first-team All-ACC player. He had two 30-point games that year only three weeks apart. Other than Charlie Scott, he was that squad's most consistent scorer.

"I like to point out to my son that Michael Jordan only had four 30-point games in his career," Bunting said, grinning. "Maybe that means I was half the player in college that Jordan was."

Bunting said his two favorite years as a Tar Heel were actually his junior year, when the Tar Heels got to the national final before losing to Lew Alcindor's UCLA squad; and his freshman year, when he played for an undefeated freshman team coached by Larry Brown. That freshman team actually beat the Tar Heel varsity in a 1966 exhibition—a varsity squad featuring both Larry Miller and Bob Lewis.

In a later rematch, the varsity would win. Smith would soon abolish the freshman/varsity game, worried that it could cause divisiveness.

"From that point on, after we had beaten the varsity that one time, people just seemed so excited in our class," Bunting said.

In the 1968 national final against UCLA, when Bunting was a junior, Smith decided to slow the game down to try to contain Alcindor.

"Dean came out in the Four Corners to start the game," Bunting said. "Everything was going great until we'd get free to go down the lane and take the layup. Alcindor swatted about the first four of them away."

North Carolina lost that game, 78-55. Smith would abandon the Four Corners during the game and try to run with UCLA, which didn't work either.

"Alcindor was in the same graduating class as we were, so everyone was probably playing for second place in those years," Bunting said.

Following his graduation, Bunting went to the ABA and played for three teams in three seasons. Smith negotiated his contract. Among Bunting's ABA teammates: Julius Erving and Rick Barry.

"Hard to believe today, but when Dr. J came into the league he was really an unknown," Bunting said. "Then he started performing these incredible human feats, just jumping over people in practice."

Between his second and third year as a pro, Bunting married his wife, Sandra, who was a nurse. They moved to Virginia, where Bunting's third year as a pro started. But he was cut by the ABA's Virginia Squires midway through that season and decided to move back to the Raleigh area and start a new life.

Although he was an education major, Bunting figured he might try to get some experience in the business world first. He interviewed with several banks and went to work for First Union's mortgage banking subsidiary, where he stayed 13 years. He's had several other jobs but settled into working for the state 11 years ago. The North Carolina Housing Finance Agency has about 90 employees in its Raleigh office.

"It's a good feeling watching the families move in," Bunting said. "There are lots of celebrations."

Bill and Sandra Bunting have one child, Will Jr., who lives in Wilmington. They frequently go to the beach to bike and golf. Sandra is still a nurse and has worked for the same group of pediatricians for 30 years.

The Buntings are steady people—folks you can count on. That was Bunting's reputation on the basketball court, too. He was always slim. But he was tough. And the fact that he picked his brother's college over his father's college back in the mid-1960s was a decision that helped make all those Final Fours possible.

BILL BUNTING BY THE NUMBERS

3	FINAL FOUR TEAMS OUT OF A POSSIBLE THREE SEASONS.
6.4	CAREER REBOUNDING AVERAGE.
18	POINTS AVERAGED AS A SENIOR, WHEN BUNTING WAS FIRST-TEAM ALL-ACC.
59.8	BUNTING'S FIELD-GOAL PERCENTAGE AS A SENIOR, WHICH WAS A UNC RECORD AT THE TIME.
193	BUNTING'S LISTED WEIGHT AT UNC (HE WAS 6-9).
1,069	CAREER POINTS AT UNC.

DICK GRUBAR

Three Straight Final Fours

D ick Grubar was going to Kentucky. That's all there was to it. A massively recruited high school basketball player out of Schenectady, New York, Grubar considered Pat Riley a close friend. Riley, two years ahead of Grubar in school, had gone to Kentucky. He had told Grubar to come along. You'll get treated well here, he said. And basketball means so much to these folks.

So Grubar was all but set for Lexington, Kentucky. Then Kentucky coach Adolph Rupp came to the Grubars' house on a recruiting visit in the mid-1960s, and the course of Grubar's life changed.

Rupp was a legend by then. And according to Grubar, Rupp never would let you forget it.

"He never talked about any of his players," Grubar said, who is now 58 years old. "All he talked about was all of his own success. It was all about him. It was unbelievable."

Rupp flew to New York to see Grubar close to Christmas and watch Grubar play in a Christmas basketball tournament. Recruiting rules were far different— and far less restrictive—back then. So Rupp sometimes traveled with a recruiting entourage, and his visit to see Grubar was one of those times.

"There must have been 15-16 people," Grubar said. "And they all decided to come to my house."

Joe and Ivy Grubar had raised a proud family that was "lower-middle class," Dick Grubar said. Joe Grubar was a welder for General Electric.

"At my house, you could maybe sit six people comfortably," Grubar said. "But Rupp brought all these people into my house, and at the time it really embarrassed my parents. They had all these people just standing around because

UNC Athletic Communications

DICK GRUBAR

1967-1969

Dick Grubar (above) was a heavily recruited high school player from the state of New York who chose UNC over Kentucky. As a sure-handed point guard, he helped the Tar Heels make it to three straight Final Fours. Grubar (right) spoke at the UNC Letterman's Reunion banquet in 2004. He served four terms on the Greensboro (North Carolina) city council during the 1990s, and remains active today in the Greensboro community and the real-estate market.

Jeffrey Camarati/UNC Athletic Communications

we didn't have chairs for them. It never even bothered Rupp, though. He just continued to talk about himself, what he'd done, and how many wins he had."

After that, Grubar decided the bluegrass might be greener elsewhere. He opened himself up to the thought of going to other schools. He thought about Boston College, then coached by Bob Cousy. He thought about Syracuse and Notre Dame. But some of those schools wanted the 6-4 Grubar to play forward, like he did in high school. He believed his future was more as a point guard.

That's where Dean Smith wanted him to play. So Grubar ended up at Chapel Hill in the late 1960s during one of the Tar Heels' first great, consistent runs in the NCAA tournament.

"I was really excited when we got him," Smith recalled. "He had such great savvy on the court."

Since freshmen were ineligible then, Grubar's class only had three years to make a mark. And it did. The Class of 1969—which also included Jim Bostick, Joe Brown, Bill Bunting, Franklin "Rusty" Clark and Gerald Tuttle—gave Smith his first three appearances in the Final Four.

None of those teams won a national championship. But all three won the ACC regular season, the ACC tournament, and the NCAA Eastern regional.

"Our best chance to win it all was probably my senior year," Grubar said, "but I didn't get to play then. I was driving in the ACC tournament against Duke and tried to plant my foot, and a Duke guy came along and just wiped me out. It was nothing illegal or anything like that. If they had arthroscopic surgery back then, maybe they could have figured out what was wrong with my knee, but they never really could."

The Tar Heels won that ACC tournament final anyway, behind Scott's 40 points, and beat Davidson for the second straight year to win the East regional. But they lost to Purdue by 27 in the national semifinals.

Grubar was never the scoring star. As the team's sure-handed point guard, he ranked fourth on the team in scoring all three of his varsity seasons. Larry Miller, Bob Lewis, Bunting and Charles Scott carried the scoring burden for those teams. But Grubar was one of the first in the Tar Heels' seemingly endless series of fine point guards. He distributed the ball, played good defense, and understood the game so well that he seemed a natural to eventually become a head coach (his hopes of an NBA career had basically been ended by the knee injury).

Said Woody Durham, the longtime radio voice of the Tar Heels and, during Grubar's time at UNC, a TV sportscaster: "I don't know if Carolina would have won the national championship in 1969. But I think their chances were a lot better than they were in 1968—until Grubar got hurt. He was the type of competitor that Dean really liked."

Added Smith: "Grubar was really underrated. He was a great college player and would have been as a pro, too, if not for that knee injury."

Like a striking number of Smith's guards over the years—including George Karl, Eddie Fogler, Jeff Lebo, Buzz Peterson, and Larry Brown—Grubar decided to try coaching. He was an assistant coach at both Virginia Commonwealth and then for six years at Florida under John Lotz, who was once Smith's assistant at UNC.

Again, the act of recruiting played a part in Grubar's life. This time, instead of pushing him toward Chapel Hill, it pushed him away from coaching.

"The hours were just brutal," Grubar said. "I'd go on the road and be gone 18 or 19 days in a row. It wasn't the way I wanted to make a living. You don't make friends as an assistant coach. You're not around enough. To create friendships, you have to be around."

Grubar decided early in his coaching career that if he didn't become a head coach by age 28, he'd try something else. He had two interviews for head coaching jobs—at Navy and East Tennessee State—but didn't much want the Navy job and didn't get the one at ETSU.

He came back to North Carolina then, living in Raleigh and working for the Department of Commerce. In 1980, he went to work for Mike Weaver, a prominent businessman in Greensboro who had interests in both construction and real estate. Grubar and Weaver are still close friends and business partners today. Grubar credits Weaver, who is also a North Carolina alumnus, with giving him a nudge toward community service.

"He is a big believer in giving back to the community," Grubar said. "He always pushed you to try and do more, to be part of boards and commissions and stuff like that. So I started doing quite a bit. After four or five years, I was on about eight different boards. I thought to myself, 'There's got to be an easier way to do this.' So that's why I ran for city council."

Grubar won four separate two-year terms on Greensboro's city council, serving from 1989-97 and helping to institute a significant recycling program while trying to manage the city's growth.

"Six years was actually enough," Grubar said. "Those last two years were like pulling teeth. I didn't really want to make it a career, and no one ought to do it anymore if they don't have higher aspirations. I decided to let new ideas come to the fore."

Grubar also has remained in touch with the UNC basketball program. He was one of the former players who urged Dean Smith to stick around long enough to best Rupp's all-time win record before retiring.

Current UNC coach Roy Williams thinks so much of Grubar that he personally selected Grubar to speak for all the players of the 1960s at the UNC basketball reunion banquet in February 2004. Grubar said during that speech that the current Tar Heel players will discover after they graduate how deeply the program resonates with everyone when they accidentally cut their finger.

"You won't bleed red then," he said. "You'll bleed blue."

Although no longer a councilman, Grubar remains involved in the Greensboro community. He led a drive to help Greensboro's minor-league baseball team, the Greensboro Grasshoppers, get a new stadium to help spur more development in the downtown area. Opponents of the stadium had succeeded in getting a public referendum on the issue, but Grubar's side won the popular vote on October 7, 2003. First Horizon Park, home of the Greensboro Grasshoppers, opened in April 2005.

"When we started on it about two months before, we were probably behind, 60 percent to 40," Grubar said. "And we ended up winning. It's about a $20-25 million project, and I think it really will help downtown."

Grubar is now a grandfather as well. His 31-year-old daughter lives in Kentucky, and he has a 16-year-old son who lives in Greensboro.

In 2004, Grubar's father passed away. Grubar went back to New York for the funeral, and while he was there he also visited the local Boys Club in Schenectady. Grubar had spent thousands of hours there as a kid, honing his basketball skills.

"I learned so much here," Grubar told the Boys Club people. "What can I do for you?"

They thought about it.

"We've never had a new scoreboard," they said.

They do now.

DICK GRUBAR BY THE NUMBERS

3.1   CAREER REBOUNDING AVERAGE.

6   YEARS AS AN ASSISTANT COACH AT FLORIDA UNDER JOHN LOTZ.

8   YEARS AS A CITY COUNCILMAN IN GREENSBORO.

10.0   CAREER SCORING AVERAGE.

13.0   SCORING AVERAGE AS A SENIOR IN 1968-69.

47.4   CAREER SHOOTING PERCENTAGE.

916   CAREER POINTS SCORED AT UNC.

Where Have You Gone?

JIM DELANY

Commissioning Excellence

He has been labeled by numerous media organizations as the "most powerful man in college sports," a behind-the-scenes wizard of handshaking and deal-making who gets everything he wants as the Big Ten's commissioner.

"It sure doesn't feel that way," said Jim Delany as we sat over a cup of coffee in Chapel Hill—the place where he was once a backup guard for two of Dean Smith's Final Four teams in the late 1960s. "I feel like we win our share on some issues. But I've had to report a lot of bad news as well."

Delany, 57, has blue-gray eyes and a rueful laugh. Both his Rolodex and his knowledge of NCAA and Big Ten structure are impressive and understandable. He was a conference commissioner at age 31 and has had an awful lot of practice by now. In 1989, Delany became only the fifth commissioner the Big Ten (founded in 1896) has ever had. Under his stewardship, the Big Ten expanded to 11 members by adding Penn State and has dramatically increased its exposure, attendance, and cash flow.

Delany has testified in front of the Senate and Congress, guided the selection of the men's NCAA basketball tournament as its chairman, and defended the controversial Bowl Championship Series. He saw two of his teams—Michigan State and Illinois—make it to the Final Four in St. Louis before the Tar Heels beat both in their run to the 2005 national championship.

Delany has a law degree from Chapel Hill and a background in NCAA enforcement. For four-plus years in the late 1970s, he was one of the men the NCAA sent out to investigate when one of its member schools was suspected of wrongdoing.

"I always say of the 10 toughest work days in my career, nine of them were at the NCAA," Delany said. "You were never very welcome on campuses. But it

JIM DELANY

1968-1970

Jim Delany (above) was a backup guard for UNC's Final Four teams in 1968 and 1969. Today, Delany (right) is the commissioner of the Big Ten conference, a post he's held since 1989, and is known as one of the most powerful men in college sports.

was a great experience. It sent me all over the country and let me deal with a lot of different situations."

He then took a leap to the Ohio Valley Conference, which made the surprising decision to hire Delany as its commissioner when he was only 31.

"I said, 'Give me a one-year contract, save yourself some money, and make a 'young' mistake," Delany said, laughing. "And they actually bought that."

For years, Delany was younger than every football coach, basketball coach, and athletic director that he supervised in the OVC. But they all quickly came to appreciate his talents and his work ethic. He drove all over the middle part of America trying to put together a TV network—and succeeded. Then he reached even higher.

Hired by the OVC in 1979, the same year that ESPN went on the air, Delany was quicker than most of his peers to recognize that ESPN would become a behemoth in college sports.

By his second year at the mid-major OVC—which is based in Nashville, Tennessee, and includes such hard-to-say-where-they-are schools like Austin Peay and Murray State—Delany had been able to put together a deal where his schools would get national, live basketball exposure in return for playing an occasional 11:30 p.m. Friday game.

"We called it *Friday Night Live*," Delany said. "It was quite an extravaganza, really. We had a New Year's Eve game. We had a game where fans were supposed to come in their pajamas—and a lot did. We did a lot of experimentation."

After 10 years at the OVC, the Big Ten hired Delany. He has worked for the conference's 11 schools ever since (the number "11" is now subtly embedded in the Big Ten's logo) out of the Big Ten offices, which are located near Chicago's O'Hare airport. Like his colleague John Swofford, the head of the Atlantic Coast Conference and also a North Carolina graduate, Delany has been instrumental in shaping the way big-time college sports are seen and played.

"Jim is remarkable," said Dean Smith. "I've sat on some NCAA committees that he's chaired, and sometimes I just think, 'Wow. This guy is pretty sharp!'"

Delany values relationships—and resilience. At one point early in his career as Big Ten commissioner, Delany said, "I probably had more adversaries than supporters."

But he persevered.

"A lot of people talk about the characteristics tied to success," Delany said. "I think resilience is the most underrated characteristic, because nobody who is successful has always been successful. There's always a dip. There's always someone who knocks you down."

Long before he rose to his current job, Delany was fighting for playing time and teaming with other members of his 1970 Tar Heel graduating class like Charlie Scott and Eddie Fogler.

Delany grew up in New Jersey, where his father was a teacher and a high school coach. Frank and Marion Delany had five children. Jim was number three. His father had played basketball at Seton Hall and his family had a long history of producing high school basketball stars for St. Benedict's Prep, a Catholic school in Newark.

Delany was a high-scoring guard on a fairly average high school team. "Carolina had a lot of highly recruited players the year I came in," Delany said. "I wasn't one of them."

Most of his recruitment interest was local. He thought about going down south, once writing a letter to the University of Virginia basketball office. Virginia never wrote him back. "That was embarrassing," Delany said.

Thankfully for Delany, the Tar Heels got interested. It didn't take long to sell Delany on the school, and he entered Chapel Hill in 1966. Delany played freshman basketball, then didn't play much as a sophomore on the Tar Heel varsity team that advanced to the 1968 Final Four. That team bulged with stars like Larry Miller, Scott, Dick Grubar, Rusty Clark, and Bill Bunting.

In his junior season, Delany thought he should start ahead of Fogler at guard, and he still remembers a conversation he had early in the season with Smith.

"Coach Smith allowed a certain level of candor in a one-on-one environment," Delany said. "I had my opportunity to talk about it, and I did. I got my chance to say my piece."

Smith didn't shake up the lineup. But he gave Delany some chances, most notably in a January 11, 1969 UNC win over Virginia Tech. Inserted into the game after several of the guards had played inconsistently, Delany made a flurry of plays to help win the game. After that, he played more often, still coming off the bench but usually getting between 15-20 minutes a game for the rest of the season. That squad also advanced to the Final Four before losing to Purdue.

Said Smith of Delany's playing days: "He's a tough rascal who would have been a great defensive halfback. Once he and a Wake Forest guy collided full speed. Jim just kind of shook it off. The Wake Forest guy was still on the floor."

Then, in 1969-70, Delany's senior year was something of a disappointment. On a team that Smith would later admit relied too heavily on Scott to carry the scoring load, the Tar Heels lost six of their final 10 games and stumbled to an 18-9 record. That would be the last North Carolina team not to win 20 games until the 2001-02 squad.

Delany ended his career with one oddly symmetrical number. He played in 73 games for UNC and made exactly 73 field goals. He averaged 3.2 points per game. Although he had a decent career, he knew the pros weren't an option. So Delany stayed in Chapel Hill and entered law school.

"Coach Smith helped me," Delany said. "I was a graduate assistant. I didn't do any coaching, but I'd referee in practice. He used to get on me for my charge/block calls."

Chuckled Smith when I read that quote to him: "Oh, that Jim.... He always had a great sense of humor."

Delany had a brief marriage during law school that produced no children. After graduating from law school, he spent the next two years serving as counsel for the North Carolina Senate Judiciary Committee and then was a staff attorney for the North Carolina Justice Department.

Then the Carolina family reached out to him again. Assistant coach Bill Guthridge had a former roommate at Kansas State who was head of the NCAA's enforcement department. Delany received an interview and was hired. That started the process that would take him to the OVC and, eventually to the Big Ten.

Delany is now married to Catherine "Kitty" Fisher Delany, who is also an attorney. Their two sons, Newman (15) and Chance (11), are both young athletes.

And their father really is one of the more powerful men in college athletics—even if he doesn't much feel like it.

JIM DELANY BY THE NUMBERS

2   FINAL FOURS PLAYED IN.

3.2   CAREER SCORING AVERAGE.

5   FREE THROWS MADE LATE IN A ONE-POINT NCAA TOURNAMENT WIN OVER DUQUESNE IN 1969.

11   ACTUAL NUMBER OF TEAMS IN THE BIG TEN CONFERENCE, OF WHICH DELANY IS THE COMMISSIONER.

31   AGE WHEN DELANY FIRST BECAME A COLLEGE COMMISSIONER (OF THE OHIO VALLEY CONFERENCE).

73   BOTH DELANY'S TOTAL NUMBER OF GAMES PLAYED FOR UNC, AND HIS TOTAL NUMBER OF FIELD GOALS.

78.0   CAREER FREE-THROW PERCENTAGE.

Where Have You Gone?

CHARLIE SCOTT

Breaking the Barrier

If you want to know how closely linked Charlie Scott is to North Carolina and vice versa, a brief lesson on the naming of sons is in order. Roy Williams, the current Tar Heel coach, thought so much of Charlie Scott's basketball skills and the way he handled being the first black scholarship athlete in any sport at UNC that Williams named his only son "Scott."

"That's quite an honor," Charlie Scott, 56, said from his home in the Atlanta area. "It makes me proud that Roy would do that. Of course, my third child is Shannon Dean Scott. His middle name is in honor of Dean Smith."

Since Scott's NBA career ended at age 33, he, his wife Trudy and their three kids have lived mostly in Atlanta and Los Angeles. Scott worked for Champion Sportswear for several years and now is in business for himself as a sports marketer. He also enjoys helping coach the AAU basketball teams of his two boys, Shaun and Shannon.

Scott's name will forever be synonymous in Chapel Hill with both integration and basketball excellence. He was the closest thing the Tar Heels ever had to a Jackie Robinson. He was also an outstanding player, averaging 22.1 points per game over the course of his career, making All-America twice and helping the Tar Heels to two Final Fours.

Said longtime Tar Heel radio voice Woody Durham, who witnessed many of Scott's exploits in person: "He really was something. He was the first Carolina player that really would compare to today's player. His build, his speed, his ability—you could take him out of the late 1960s and drop him into today's game, and he wouldn't miss a beat."

Scott's father was a cab driver in New York, and Charlie was the first person in his family to attend college. He grew up mostly in Harlem, but showed

UNC Athletic Communications

CHARLIE SCOTT

1968-1970

The first African American to be awarded a scholarship at UNC, Charlie Scott (above) averaged 22.1 points per game over the course of his career and was a two-time All-America selection. He went on to average nearly 18 points per game in the NBA. Today, Scott (right)—shown here with Dean Smith—works as a sports marketer and coaches AAU basketball in Georgia.

enough basketball talent there that he transferred to Laurinburg Institute in North Carolina for most of his high school career. Some of his friends had gone there and liked it.

"That would be like someone going to Oak Hill in Virginia today," Scott said of the prestigious prep school. "It had a well-known basketball program. I knew my family wouldn't be able to afford college, so a scholarship was going to have to be my ticket."

The first coach to show much of an interest in Scott was Lefty Driesell. Driesell was the young coach at Davidson at the time, where he was building a very good team at the private school. He wanted Scott to be his centerpiece, and Scott at first agreed.

"I took a great liking to Lefty," Scott said. "I went to Davidson for summer camp. He was the first coach to recruit me and the first one to offer me a scholarship. I had applied for early admission to Davidson and been accepted."

Grades weren't going to be a problem for Scott. Out of a graduating class of "about 70," he said, he was the valedictorian at Laurinburg. But his high school coach tried to persuade him that he should explore the recruitment process more fully. Scott went to see Duke, N.C. State, Wake Forest and North Carolina, among others, and came away most impressed with Chapel Hill.

Eventually, Scott would change his mind and decide on North Carolina. Much of the reasoning came from something Driesell couldn't control: Scott felt like Chapel Hill was a more open, accepting place in the late 1960s than Davidson. It may have helped that his recruiting visit occurred during a gorgeous spring weekend that included a concert by both The Temptations and Smokey Robinson & the Miracles.

It definitely helped that Dean Smith took Scott to church with him during his official visit—something no other coach had done. The visit to Olin T. Binkley Memorial Baptist made a lasting impression on Scott.

"I wanted him to see Binkley, because we were one of the few churches around that was fully integrated at the time," Smith said in our interview for this book. "I wanted him to know he could feel comfortable there. I didn't force him to go—I just asked him, 'Do you want to go to church, Charles?' He said he did, so we went."

Smith also called Scott "Charles" from the beginning, rather than the more familiar "Charlie" that everyone else used, because Scott said he preferred that.

If Scott was going to break a color barrier, he decided he would rather do it at Chapel Hill with Dean Smith. Driesell was heartbroken.

"Lefty now lives in Atlanta, too," Scott said, "and he still talks about it. He thinks things would have been different if I had come there. We beat Davidson twice to get to the Final Four in the late 1960s, and he believes if I'd gone to Davidson, that would have been him in the Final Four instead. I understand what he's saying. I'm not sure he ever quite got over it."

In one of the most well-known recruiting stories in ACC circles, Driesell showed up to see Scott one last time to try to re-recruit him after Scott had changed his mind and committed to Carolina.

"They say he jumped out of some bushes to talk to me," Scott said, "but it wasn't quite like that. I had called him to tell him I was going to Carolina, but I had only talked to his wife. He came to see me one more time to see if he could change my mind. He got a friend of mine to take a walk with me to this place off-campus, and then he did come out from behind some bushes to talk to me. I listened, but I was going to Carolina."

Carolina will never forget Scott. On the road, he was able to cope with the racist chanting he occasionally heard. And at Chapel Hill, he found a comfortable home.

"It was a conscious decision by me to stay in the South rather than go up North to play," Scott said. "It was the late 1960s, and a lot of blacks, including me, were aware of their responsibilities. In those times, if you could do something, you did. I wanted to break the color barrier."

Since Scott grew up mostly in New York and had taken public transportation everywhere, he didn't know how to drive when he got to Chapel Hill. But he found little problem getting rides to where he needed to go.

"I was realistic, accepting that some bad things were going to happen," Scott said. "On campus, I really didn't feel bias or bigotry. I never felt unwanted."

As a sophomore, Scott joined a team that had already been to one Final Four, in 1967, keyed by players like Larry Miller, Dick Grubar, and Bill Bunting. Scott arrived to take the place of the high-scoring Bobby Lewis and immediately fit in, helping the Tar Heels go 28-4.

"That was probably the best team I was on at Carolina," Scott said. "But UCLA was absolutely tremendous that season. We had a better chance to beat them in my junior year, when they weren't quite as good."

However, the Tar Heels only faced UCLA in the Final Four in Scott's sophomore year. Carolina made it to the NCAA final that season, but UCLA demolished them, 78-55. Lew Alcindor—who would later change his name to Kareem Abdul-Jabbar—scored 34 points and pulled down 16 rebounds for UCLA.

Scott played for the U.S. Olympic team that summer, helping the Hank Iba-coached squad to a gold medal, and returned to Carolina full of confidence for his junior year.

And the 1968-69 Tar Heels never would have made it back to the Final Four without him. In those years a team had to win the ACC tournament to qualify for the NCAAs. North Carolina was facing Duke in the ACC tournament final, and Scott took over the second half against Duke. Guard Dick Grubar had blown out his knee in the first half, and the Tar Heels looked to be done. The phrase "Great Scott" was never more appropriate.

"[Then-Duke coach] Vic Bubas would say later in an interview that he looked over at the Tar Heel bench," Woody Durham recalled, "and everyone looked beat. Except for Scott."

Shooting anytime he was open and many times when he wasn't, Scott rallied North Carolina from nine points down to an 11-point win. The 6-6 junior ended up with 40 points (28 in the second half) and made 17 of his 23 shots from the field.

"That game has to be the highlight of my college career," Scott said. "It always felt so good to beat Duke."

Said Roy Williams, who was then a student at Chapel Hill: "What Charlie Scott did in that game was one of the greatest college basketball performances of all time."

Despite being an All-American, Scott lost out on ACC Player of the Year to South Carolina's John Roche in a vote he believed was racially motivated. Scott was the ACC tournament MVP, however.

Scott thought briefly about not playing in the NCAA tournament to showcase the slight he felt he received from those who voted for Roche. But he was talked out of that partly by assistant coach John Lotz, who was such a close friend of Scott's that he ended up being the best man in Scott's wedding.

"I still miss him every day," said Scott of Lotz, who passed away in 2001.

It was a good thing Scott played against Davidson. In an Elite Eight NCAA game, Scott scored 32 points against Driesell, including a long jumper at the buzzer to win a thriller, 87-85. That jumper resulted in an explosion of joy from the Carolina bench—Smith put both hands aloft, clenching his fists, and assistant coach Bill Guthridge jumped at least two feet in the air.

Once the Tar Heels got to the Final Four, however, they played poorly. They were creamed by a Purdue team featuring Rick Mount, 92-65, and didn't get a shot at UCLA.

Scott's final Carolina team as a senior (1969-70) wasn't as strong due to graduation losses. He averaged 27.1 points per game on a team that didn't qualify for the NCAAs.

"I think I did a bad job that year," said Dean Smith. "We were down a little, and most people didn't pick us to be great, but we probably relied too much on one player. I'll blame myself for that and nobody else."

Scott attributes some of his greatness in college to his amazing first step, but more to his work ethic and competitive drive. He also worked hard in the classroom, earning Academic All-America once.

"When I finished a test, I would want the teacher to mark it right then," Scott said. "I wanted to see how I did. I couldn't wait to get grades back. That's just the way I was."

From Chapel Hill, it was on to the pros. Scott began in the ABA and absolutely dominated with the Virginia Squires, averaging 27.1 points as the league's Rookie of the Year and then 34.6 in his second season. Scott then jumped leagues and followed Billy Cunningham as the second great NBA player to be coached by Smith (Bob McAdoo would be the third and Bobby Jones the fourth).

Scott played for Phoenix from 1972-75 and then for Boston for most of the next three seasons. He finished his career in Denver in 1980, averaging nearly 18 points per game in the NBA.

His favorite team? The 1975-76 Celtics that won the NBA championship.

"That was a team that thought it was the best," said Scott, who averaged 17.6 points for the Celtics that season. "We had Don Nelson, John Havlicek, Jo Jo White, Paul Silas—they were intelligent players and great players. We really felt we had no weakness."

Scott has maintained close ties with his university, and his children have visited Chapel Hill often enough to fall in love with the school. His oldest child is his daughter, Simone, and she's nearing college age.

"When you ask her the top three choices on her list, she says, 'Carolina, Carolina, Carolina,'" Scott said. "All my kids have their heart set on going there. And why not? It's a really special place."

CHARLIE SCOTT BY THE NUMBERS

0   BLACK SCHOLARSHIP ATHLETES AT UNC BEFORE SCOTT.

1   OLYMPIC GOLD MEDAL (1968 IN MEXICO CITY).

2   TIME ALL-AMERICA AT UNC.

7.1   CAREER REBOUNDING AVERAGE.

22.1   CAREER SCORING AVERAGE.

33   HONORED UNIFORM NUMBER AT UNC; ANTAWN JAMISON LATER RETIRED IT.

40   POINTS AGAINST DUKE IN THE ACC TOURNAMENT FINAL IN 1969.

2,007   CAREER POINTS SCORED AT UNC (FIFTH ALL-TIME).

Where Have You Gone?

DAVID
CHADWICK

God's Unconditional Love

David Chadwick stood on the second level of the gorgeous sanctuary at
Forest Hill Church in Charlotte. Surrounding him were 2,000 theater-style
seats. Below him was a huge stage dotted with more than a dozen musical
instruments. Ready to drop from the ceiling were the video screens used at every
service, often to play a clip from a current movie or TV show.

There was no pulpit.

Chadwick, the senior pastor at one of the largest churches in the Carolinas,
doesn't use one. The six-foot-eight former Tar Heel basketball player prefers to
walk around while delivering his message of God's love to the Forest Hill
congregation, which averages 3,500 people in attendance every weekend.

"This is not your Mama's church," Chadwick said, grinning. "And that's
because we're not trying to reach your Mama—although I'm sure she's very
nice."

In 25 years, Chadwick has transformed a sleepy church into a sprawling
place that looks like a college campus and has spread Chadwick's central
message—God loves us all unconditionally—to tens of thousands.

"I love to preach," Chadwick said. "I have a gift of communication, and I
love to communicate truth to people, mostly about God's grace and
unconditional love. When I see people's eyes light up when they realize that
God's not out to punish them, He's not out to get them, that God loves them so
much that he was willing to die for their sins—that makes my heart happier than
you can possibly imagine! I love to see them grasp grace and move from being
lost, destitute, hurting, to free, joyful, life-giving souls who can then give of
themselves to other people."

With his piercing blue eyes and shock of gray hair, Chadwick, 56, has
become something of a multimedia star in Charlotte (although, like Dean

DAVID CHADWICK

1969-1971

As a 6-8 post player, David Chadwick (above) averaged 8.7 points per game as a senior, and scored 30 points against Clemson during the same year. Today, Chadwick (right) is the senior pastor at Forest Hill Church in Charlotte and has also written five books.

Smith, he prefers to bat away credit). Chadwick is a regular on WBT radio in Charlotte, hosting his own weekly radio program and also offering daily one-minute "Moments of Hope" to the listeners. Those "Moments of Hope," which began after the 9-11 tragedy, have been collected into a series of three books.

Chadwick also has written a book about his relationship with his father, who was also a well-loved minister, entitled *My Father, My Friend*. As the father of three young boys, that book has personally been helpful to me, with its chapter headings like "Kids Spell Love T-I-M-E" and "You're Always a Parent, No Matter What Age They Are."

But the first book among the five Chadwick has written is probably his most well-known: *The 12 Leadership Principles of Dean Smith*.

Whenever he is asked about this book, Smith likes to say he didn't know he had exactly 12 leadership principles because he had never counted them. But Chadwick actually did a fine job breaking down Smith's philosophy in a 1999 book that sold more than 40,000 copies. (Smith would also delve deeply into this topic in his own book *The Carolina Way* in 2004). Taking Smith's admonition not to deify him in the book seriously, Chadwick wrote chapters like "The Reciprocal Law of Loyalty" but also one entitled "Making Failure Your Friend."

Chadwick was not a star at Carolina. But he was a solid post player who has taken Smith's mostly secular messages and applied them to his life and his church in countless ways.

"If Forest Hill is successful, I'd say it's largely because of what Coach Smith taught me by playing under him, and also by observation, over the last several decades on how to lead," Chadwick said.

Chadwick was born in Winston-Salem, North Carolina, in 1949, the son of Howard and Helen Chadwick. Howard Chadwick was a Moravian minister at that time, but in 1953 he got the call to become a Presbyterian minister. He served Westminster Presbyterian in Charlotte for 10 years, from 1953-63, before moving the family to another church in Kansas City after Chadwick's seventh-grade year. The family then moved again after David's high school sophomore year to Orlando, Florida, so his father could minister to the First Presbyterian church there.

"Between my sophomore and junior years [in high school] I grew from maybe 6-5, 155 pounds to 6-7 1/2 and 185 pounds," Chadwick said. "Suddenly, I got more coordinated, too. And I started to get to play more of basketball—a game I loved to play but hadn't been very good at until then."

North Carolina recruited Chadwick out of Florida, and he entered Chapel Hill in 1967.

His first year on the varsity came on the 1968-69 Final Four team, where he was a reserve who played sparingly. Chadwick's playing time gradually increased as a junior.

Then he played a lot as a senior on a surprisingly good 26-6 team. He started about half the games and scored in double figures numerous times, including in the Tar Heels' 1971 NIT championship win over Georgia Tech, when Chadwick had 14 points and 12 rebounds. Chadwick still has a newspaper clipping chronicling that victory from a New York newspaper on his office wall at Forest Hill, headlined "NC Wins NIT Title, 84-66."

(Interestingly, one of the pictures in Chadwick's office is an autographed photo of Duke coach Mike Krzyzewski. It's more of a conversation piece than anything else—a member at Forest Hill arranged for Coach K to sign it and send it to Chadwick as a practical joke. It reads: "Great Player, Wrong Team!!")

After his career as a Tar Heel ended, Chadwick still wanted to play. He was one of the first North Carolina players to go overseas to play pro basketball, spending one year in Belgium and two years in France.

"All of that time I wondered where I was going to end up," Chadwick said. "When I came back, I knew I had to grow up, quit playing basketball, and find something to do with my life."

With the aid of John Lotz, a former UNC assistant who had become the head coach at Florida, Chadwick became a graduate assistant for the Gators basketball program for two years while getting a master's degree in counseling. The ministry still wasn't a serious consideration for him.

"Then, at the end of the second year of my time in Gainesville, Florida, I had a real profound experience with the Lord," Chadwick said. "It was just one of those real confusing times in my life. I had a girl I thought I was going to marry, and it didn't work out. The Lord drove me onto my knees one night in my Gainesville apartment, and I really sensed his overwhelming call to the ministry.

"I had not previously responded to that call, I think, because that was my dad's calling, not my calling. But I heard something deep in my heart."

Chadwick moved to Atlanta and completed two degrees at Columbia Theological Seminary. While there, he met his future wife, Marilynn, on a blind date. "I had had so many bad blind dates I had sworn off of them," Chadwick said.

It was a good thing he made room for one more. He and Marilynn had a whirlwind courtship—they were engaged within three months and married within nine.

In 1980, Chadwick was contacted about an opening for senior pastor at Forest Hill, which at the time drew about 150 people for Sunday worship.

"There was one baby in the nursery," Chadwick said. "That baby is now on our staff here."

Chadwick's vision was that church was too often dull or irrelevant for young people and that he would embrace popular culture—contemporary music, movies, and television—as a way of bringing the message of God.

"It's what missionaries do," Chadwick said. "If you go to Ethiopia, you learn their style, their culture, and their language. Then you take the priceless, timeless message of the Gospel and give it to them in a way they can understand. That's what we do here."

David and Marilynn Chadwick now have three children of their own. Their daughter, Bethany, goes to Wake Forest and showed up for one Saturday-night service after Wake Forest beat UNC in early 2005 dressed entirely in black and gold.

"You can imagine how disruptive it was to my soul to announce to the congregation where she was going to college," Chadwick laughed.

His middle child, David Banner Chadwick, is six-foot-seven and a fine high school basketball player. Unfortunately, he has also had to go through a couple of knee injuries. Chadwick enlisted Dean Smith to offer his son some encouragement after one of those and Smith did so, although he first wanted to know about the young man's grades. The Chadwicks' third child, Michael, is 10.

After 25 years at Forest Hill (www.foresthill.org), Chadwick believes he will probably be at the innovative church for the rest of his ministry. He has passed up opportunities to go elsewhere in favor of staying in Charlotte, where he can continue to try to change lives.

Said Chadwick: "Strangely, God uses a broken person like me—with all of my ineptness, foibles, and fallacies—to change other people's lives with this incredible gospel of unconditional love."

DAVID CHADWICK BY THE NUMBERS

5.9   CAREER SCORING AVERAGE.

6   SHOTS HIT WITHOUT MISSING IN ACC TOURNAMENT 1971 SEMIFINAL AGAINST VIRGINIA.

8.7   SCORING AVERAGE AS A SENIOR.

22   POINTS IN NIT QUARTERFINAL GAME AGAINST PROVIDENCE IN 1971.

30   CAREER HIGH IN POINTS, AGAINST CLEMSON DURING SENIOR SEASON.

58.6   SHOOTING PERCENTAGE AS A SENIOR.

434   CAREER POINTS AT UNC.

LEE DEDMON

The Principal of Success

At a shade under seven feet tall, Lee Dedmon isn't your average high school principal.

That's okay, as he doesn't lead an average high school.

Highland School of Technology, located in a working-class neighborhood of Gastonia, North Carolina, was the first public high school in the state to be named a School of Excellence. That distinction came about when more than 90 percent of the school's students scored at or above grade level on end-of-course tests.

The magnet school is so popular in Gaston County that for the 2005-06 school year, 625 students applied for the 145 available spots open to entering freshmen.

When you walk in the front door, one of the first things you see is a well-displayed quote. The inspirational quotes change for every school day. The similarity between those quotes and the "Thought of the Day" that was included on the written plan for every Dean Smith practice at North Carolina is no coincidence. Dedmon tries to build his school much like Smith built his team in Chapel Hill. Dedmon has even had former Tar Heel and current pastor David Chadwick visit to talk to his faculty regarding the book Chadwick wrote about Smith's leadership skills.

Dedmon has been a principal since 1983 and has presided over Highland School of Technology since shortly after it opened in 2000. Students choose from one of three emphases—Communication and Information Technology; Health Sciences and Biomedical Technology; and Manufacturing/Engineering and Graphics.

LEE DEDMON

1969-1971

Center Lee Dedmon (above), who averaged 11.4 points and 8.2 rebounds over the course of his career, was instrumental in the Tar Heels' run to the 1971 NIT championship. Today, Dedmon (right) stands tall—at a shade under seven feet— as the principal at Highland School of Technology.

"What I enjoy about being a principal has always been consistent—it's the different challenges that come every day," Dedmon said as we talked in his office. "It's very similar to being a police officer or a stockbroker. I have no clue what is going to happen during the day. I know the general outline of the day. But the exciting part is that something pops up every day, both good and bad."

That's like a basketball game, isn't it? You know roughly how long the game will go, when it will start, and how many players will play at a time. But the rest is all guesswork.

Most of the 550 kids at Highland undoubtedly don't know that their principal was once co-MVP of the 1971 ACC tournament—an honor he won despite being involved in the well-known jump ball that lost the game. But many do know exactly how tall Dedmon is. That's because Dedmon, rather than shy away from questions about his imposing height, has encouraged them. With his deep voice and powerful build, Dedmon knows that he looks a bit intimidating to a ninth-grader. To counteract that, he tells all of the students that his exact height is 6-11 and 3/4.

Every day in the hallway, Dedmon will ask a couple of kids exactly how tall he is. If they get it right, he laughs, pulls out a dollar bill and hands it to them.

Dean Smith, incidentally, listed Dedmon at only 6-10. But Smith was well known for listing his players as slightly shorter than they actually were, trying to get opponents to literally underestimate them. Dedmon understands psychology, especially from a teenage perspective. He once came close to training to be an FBI agent, and even now he relishes the challenge of trying to figure out the occasional mystery that pops up at every school.

"I like the investigative part of being a principal, too," he said.

At age 55, Dedmon could retire with substantial state benefits. He has been in education for more than 30 years, most of those as a principal at Gaston County middle or high schools. But he plans to work at least a couple of years longer, because he cares about the job and thinks that he can still be valuable to kids today.

"I really like what I do," Dedmon said. "There are some days I'd rather be playing golf or hunting, but the majority of time I don't have problem getting up in the morning. I'm concerned about the drugs in schools and the violence that kids see, sure. But overall, kids are basically the same as they've always been. They just have different toys."

Dedmon grew up in Baltimore, where his father was a 39-year veteran of the Baltimore police department. He and Chadwick were in the same freshman class at Chapel Hill.

"Nothing ever seemed to bother Lee much on the court," Smith recalled.

Dedmon was a reserve as a sophomore and then started his final two seasons, averaging a solid 11.4 points for his career. As a senior, he was instrumental in the Tar Heels' 1971 run to the NIT championship.

Still, there's no getting around this: Mention the name "Lee Dedmon" to older Tar Heel fans, and the first thing they think of is "The Tip."

"It's amazing that you can do something wrong and people remember you for it," Dedmon said.

With three seconds to play in the 1971 ACC tournament final, the Tar Heels led their then-bitter rival, South Carolina, 51-50. The Gamecocks had the ball and were trying to score, but Dedmon tied up Kevin Joyce under the basket for a jump ball.

Smith called timeout. If the nearly seven-foot Dedmon outjumped the 6-3 Joyce and tipped the ball to the right person, it would be very difficult for North Carolina to lose. Smith would later write in his 1999 memoir, *A Coach's Life*, that during the timeout he made a decision "that I later wished I could take back." Instead of having Dedmon tip the ball to another tall player, Bill Chamberlain, as he would usually do, Smith asked Dedmon to tip it to guard George Karl.

"I told everyone else where to line up—but I failed to make it clear to one player," Smith wrote without identifying the player in question. "When a player doesn't know where to go, it's the coach's mistake."

All Dedmon remembers about the play now is this: "I really think I tipped it the wrong way. I've looked at the tape numerous times. But Kevin [Joyce] thinks he got the tip. It's one of those debates you'll never know."

Ultimately, Dedmon and Joyce combined somehow to knock the ball toward the South Carolina basket. Neither Karl nor anyone else in Carolina blue grabbed it. Instead, the Gamecocks' Tom Owens came up with the ball and laid it in for a shocking 52-51 win.

That sent North Carolina to the NIT—a much better tournament back then compared to what it is now but still the second choice. South Carolina got the coveted NCAA bid—in those years the ACC was allowed only one entry.

Said Woody Durham, longtime radio voice of the Tar Heels: "That game should never have come down to that jump ball. The Tar Heels missed so many free throws late in that game."

Dedmon has refused to brood about the play over the years. Smith taking the blame repeatedly has helped. And Dedmon realizes that he played an excellent tournament overall, hence the co-MVP award.

It also helped that Penn bounced South Carolina out of the NCAA tournament in the first round. There was bad blood between the two Carolina teams—a South Carolina player had reportedly cursed at Smith after the ACC fianl—and the Tar Heel players got some retribution after that Gamecock loss.

"We sent them flowers," Dedmon said, laughing. The Tar Heels would go on to win four games and the NIT. Dedmon still wears the ring from that championship.

Dedmon would play a single year in the pros, for Utah in the ABA. He had intentions of playing some more in Europe. But in the offseason, he came through the Gastonia area (20 miles from Charlotte) with his first wife, found a teaching job, and never left. He coached basketball for four years as well, but stopped doing that as he began advancing through the administrative ranks.

Dedmon and his second wife, Marilyn, have been married for 17 years. Dedmon has a son who is working on his Ph.D. at Cambridge in biochemistry. His daughter goes to Texas A&M. He also has a stepson.

To watch Dedmon do his work as a principal is to see a man who walks the halls with words of encouragement, a sharp eye for valid hall passes and a few dollar bills in his front right pocket. It's easy to tell that Dedmon's life has stretched far beyond one jump ball, and far into the lives of thousands of kids.

LEE DEDMON BY THE NUMBERS

2   YEARS HE LED UNC IN REBOUNDING.

8.2   CAREER REBOUNDING AVERAGE.

11.4   CAREER SCORING AVERAGE.

23   POINTS DEDMON ONCE SCORED AGAINST A FLORIDA STATE
          TEAM LED BY DAVE COWENS.

48.1   CAREER SHOOTING PERCENTAGE.

88   ASSISTS AS A SENIOR (SECOND ON THE TEAM THAT SEASON).

1,019   CAREER POINTS.

Where Have You Gone?

STEVE PREVIS

A Life in London

He has spent the night in a Mexican prison on a trumped-up charge. He has lived in the Arabian Gulf. He is now a permanent resident of London, where he has lived for the past 13 years. Of all the former Tar Heel basketball players chronicled in this book, Steve Previs is undoubtedly the most international. With an adventurous spirit and a gift for high finance, Previs, 55, has traveled the world.

But the travel has only accentuated to Previs what a special place the small town of Chapel Hill is, particularly due to the college basketball program located there.

"Those were four of the most unbelievable years ever," Previs said. "If I could ever give the ultimate gift to anybody, I'd give them four years of Carolina basketball. I wouldn't trade that experience for a billion dollars, and that's the gospel truth."

That statement sounds like hyperbole until you realize that Previs is one of the few men who can probably grasp how much a billion dollars is actually worth. Previs trades large blocks of stock for the London branch of Jefferies & Company, an investment bank and equity trading firm headquartered in New York. He lives in central London and also owns an English country home. He doesn't own a car, calls the subway "the tube" and has grown thoroughly accustomed to the British way of life. Previs was in England when terrorists' bombs raked the city's mass transit system on June 7, 2005, killing more than 50 people. Previs wasn't hurt. Like his country men, he vowed to continue what he called "life as usual" to show the terrorists they had not won.

"You have to go with the flow in any foreign country," Previs said. "You're a guest of that country, and you have to act as a guest. You don't try to impose your own culture on an existing culture."

STEVE PREVIS

1970-1972

Steve Previs, who Bill Guthridge called a "great leader and a hard worker," was twice named the team's top defender by UNC coaches. The Tar Heels went 70-20 during Previs's three years on the varsity. Previs (right) is now a permanent resident of England and works in finance.

That doesn't mean Previs has become an oh-so-proper Brit. Long renowned by many in Chapel Hill for his dead-on impersonations—"He did the best Lefty Driesell I ever heard and a really good Dean Smith, too," said longtime Tar Heel radio voice Woody Durham—Previs still likes a good practical joke. Case in point: We were supposed to do our interview for this book one afternoon at 2:30 p.m., and Previs said he wanted to call me from London rather than vice versa. My phone rang at 2:28 p.m., and a man with a deep Southern accent was on the phone. The man started to complain about my latest sports column for *The Charlotte Observer* and threatened me with all sorts of bodily harm.

"I don't have time for this because I've got a phone interview to do in a couple of minutes!" I said angrily, hanging up the phone.

Seconds later, the phone rang.

"Gotcha," Previs said sweetly.

Previs grew up in Bethel Park, Pennsylvania, the son of Steve and Eleanor Previs. He was a hard-nosed guard from a state that produced several very good players for Carolina in that era in addition to himself, like Larry Miller, Dennis Wuycik and George Karl. Recruited heavily by Duke and Boston College as well, Previs also considered both those schools. But Dean Smith ended the recruiting battle one night when he took Previs and his father to a nearby restaurant.

"Coach Smith said, 'We really want you to come to Chapel Hill,'" Previs remembered. "I said, 'Coach, don't worry.'"

On his own, Smith decided this comment constituted a commitment.

"He said, 'Congratulations!' and shook my hand," Previs said, laughing. "He was such a closer."

Remembered Bill Guthridge: "Steve's class was the first one I really helped recruit as well. He came from such a nice family, and it was a pleasure for all of us involved. We all know that Dean Smith has such an unbelievable memory, and I still think today you could drop Dean down in Pennsylvania and he could find the Previs house."

Previs and Karl, who became a well-known NBA coach, played together in the Carolina backcourt for much of their careers. Said Durham, whose first year as radio voice of the Tar Heels was Previs's senior year of 1971-72: "If there was a loose ball, Steve was going to go get it, as long as he could outfight George Karl for it."

Although he scored a modest 5.6 points per game in 89 career contests, Previs was known as a hustler and a defensive stopper. Smith often praised him publicly for doing the little things that don't show up in the basketball boxscores.

Previs played on the 1972 Final Four team, as well as the squad that won the NIT championship in 1971. He was a floor leader on those teams, and his parents became well known to many in the locker room as well. Both were fixtures at many of his games.

"I remember we called his father 'Big Steve,' and he and his wife later became great friends of ours," recalled Durham. "Once Big Steve walked into the locker room and gave his son a big embrace. I remember thinking at the time I'd never seen a father and son hug quite like that. It's still a wonderful, unique relationship."

Previs had dreams of playing pro basketball and did play one season for the ABA's Carolina Cougars in 1972-73. The lefty was a reserve on a team that starred Billy Cunningham, who would be the ABA's league MVP that season.

But the Cougars' owner, Tedd Munchak, had far bigger plans for Previs. Munchak sensed Previs had a head for business—his father, Big Steve, was very successful in the mutual-fund game—and decided Previs would be of more value working for him off the court rather than on it.

"Tedd walked right out onto the floor when I was warming up in training camp and said, 'When are you going to get a job?'" Previs recalled. "He wanted me to come work for him, and I did."

Munchak had all sorts of business interests, and he started training Previs in several. Munchak also had a huge cattle ranch outside Rome, Georgia, and for a while he turned Previs into a cowboy.

"I literally went from playing basketball to sinking fenceposts, stringing barbed wire and chasing stray calves through the woods on a horse," Previs said. "It was the toughest job I've ever had in my life."

Munchak also taught Previs how to read a financial statement and how to dissect a company's finances as well. Previs's role quickly increased. He soon had left the cowboy boots at home and was running a snack-food company owned by Munchak. After working for Munchak in both Chicago and Puerto Rico, Previs was assigned by Munchak to supervise the construction of a meat-processing plant in Mexico.

"It was literally in the middle of nowhere and 20 minutes from the nearest telephone," Previs said.

The factory was built, and it was beautiful. But Previs found out that some Mexican officials wanted to be heavily "involved" to let it run successfully. Although at this point Previs spoke fluent Spanish, he couldn't reason his way out of it. Apparently, some of the Mexicans believe putting Previs in jail could force Munchak's company to pay out some serious bribe money.

"One day two immigration officials arrested me and took me to jail on trumped-up charges that I had humiliated a person so badly in the plant that he was unable to have sex with his wife anymore," Previs said. "A guy literally put a military .45 to the back of my neck. They took my passport, all of my money and my identification."

Previs did manage to convince the authorities to let him call his attorney. Thanks to some friends in higher places, he was released the next day. Previs came back to the States and decided he would pursue a career in finance like his father. He worked in Greensboro for awhile and later found a banking job on the island of Bahrain, in the Arabian Gulf.

"I went over there in 1987, stayed for three years and got out just before the Gulf War," Previs said. "It was actually a beautiful place."

In 1992, he moved to London, where he has worked in finance ever since. The most difficult time in his life, Previs said, occurred in London in 1996. He had been married to his college sweetheart, Leslie Hibbard, for seven years. The two had gotten a divorce, but then had later fallen back in love and planned to be remarried. Then Leslie died of a sudden stroke at age 45.

"I almost gave up," Previs said softly. "I was really losing it. I felt like I couldn't carry on. But then I kept thinking, 'What would Coach Smith think about you if he knew you were doing this? He didn't spend all that time teaching you to be mentally tough for nothing!' I still don't think he knows how much that helped me. I tell you what, I love him so much."

Previs has no children. However, he does have a serious girlfriend in London, Connie, who is a writer.

"She's an amputee—she had her leg amputated when she was 13 years old—and she is absolutely one of the most remarkable people I've ever met," Previs said. "She's my princess."

Previs has kept in contact with Smith over the years and is still amazed by his good fortune at choosing Carolina as a high school senior in a Pennsylvania restaurant.

"Coach Smith is a person who—if you're very, very lucky—you get to meet for five minutes in your life," Previs said. "And I got to be with him for four years. Just think about that."

STEVE PREVIS BY THE NUMBERS

1   GAME MISSED IN THREE SEASONS.

2   TIMES THAT UNC COACHES SELECTED PREVIS AS HIS TEAM'S TOP DEFENDER (1971 AND '72).

5.6   CAREER SCORING AVERAGE.

10   CAREER HIGH IN ASSISTS, AGAINST N.C. STATE.

13   YEARS LIVED IN LONDON, WHERE PREVIS IS NOW A PERMANENT RESIDENT.

22   CAREER HIGH IN POINTS, AGAINST WAKE FOREST.

286   CAREER ASSISTS.

BOB McADOO

One Year of Mc–Magic

It's a common issue today for every elite high school and college basketball player. The question is always the same: Should I jump to the NBA early, or should I remain in school? The first player in North Carolina history to make the leap was Bob McAdoo, who played just one season for the Tar Heels. In 1971-72, McAdoo was a junior-college transfer and both the leading scorer and rebounder on the Tar Heels' 1972 Final Four team.

With one season of eligibility remaining, and with coach Dean Smith's blessing, McAdoo left early for the NBA immediately after that season. And McAdoo, 54, is still in the NBA. He has spent the past 10 seasons as an assistant coach for the Miami Heat. His most recent assignment has been to work closely with Shaquille O'Neal. In their first season together, in 2004-05, McAdoo, Shaq, and the Heat reached the Eastern Conference finals before narrowly losing a seven-game series to the defending champs, the Detroit Pistons.

Even though it was 33 years ago, McAdoo still remembers the one moment that made him decide to go pro.

McAdoo's father, Robert, was a carpenter. His mother, Vandalia, was a schoolteacher. Coach Smith had told McAdoo that if he could get paid at least $100,000 for his NBA rookie season—huge money back then in the NBA—he should skip his senior season at Chapel Hill and leave early.

"So, sure enough, that $100,000 figure came up," McAdoo recalled. "I could get that, and I would get that. But there were competing forces in my house. My mother, being a teacher, she was dead set against it. She didn't want to hear anything about it. My father, though—he saw that $100,000 contract. And he called me into a room in the house, and he pulled out a check stub out of his

UNC Athletic Communications

BOB McADOO

1972

Bob McAdoo (above) led the Tar Heels in scoring and rebounding during his one season at UNC. He left for the NBA—with Dean Smith's blessing—following North Carolina's trip to the Final Four in 1972. Today, McAdoo (right) works as assistant coach with the Miami Heat. He tutors the Heat's big men, including Shaquille O'Neal (pictured).

Miami Heat

drawer. The stub showed what he made the year before as a carpenter –$10,000. When he showed me that, I made up my mind right there."

Dean Smith would later note in his 1999 biography, *A Coach's Life*, that he "heartily approved" of McAdoo's decision.

"By way of comparison, I was making $18,000 a year at the time," Smith wrote.

McAdoo, obviously, made the correct decision. He was elected to the Basketball Hall of Fame in 2000 after a spectacular career in which he led the NBA in scoring for three consecutive years from 1973-76 and appeared in five straight all-star games. For his NBA career, he averaged 22.1 points and 9.4 rebounds a game—a smooth, 6-9 big man who could shoot both inside and out.

"I took what the defense gave me," McAdoo said. "If they shaded me right, I'd go left. If they gave me too much room, I'd shoot a jumper. If they crowded me, I drove. I was just a basketball player."

Although he spent only one season in Chapel Hill as the Tar Heels' first JUCO transfer, McAdoo remains very loyal to the North Carolina program. He has sent his children to North Carolina basketball and tennis camps for years— McAdoo's primary game is tennis now, and several of his kids are accomplished players.

McAdoo's primary job with the Miami Heat is to work with the Heat's big men. That means he started closely supervising Shaq in the 2004-05 season, which has both its positive side (Shaq's physical skills) and its negative side (McAdoo also is responsible for improving Shaq's horrid free-throw shooting). McAdoo lives in Miami with his wife, Patrizia, and four of McAdoo's six children.

"I'm into being happy, and I'm happy with what I'm doing now," McAdoo said. "That's the way most of my life has gone. I don't worry about things. I don't politic for a head-coaching job. People fight like crazy for any job coaching in the NBA, and I've got one of them."

Although McAdoo grew up in Greensboro, only about an hour away from Chapel Hill, it's an upset that he attended North Carolina at all. He ended up being one of the first black basketball players at UNC, following the lead of Charlie Scott and Bill Chamberlain, but it could easily have been otherwise.

"Even though Carolina was close by, that school was never on my parents' lips," McAdoo said. "Growing up in Greensboro, we watched the CIAA [the Central Intercollegiate Athletic Association, a black-college league located primarily in North Carolina]. My father took me to watch Earl Monroe. I was recruited by "Big House" Gaines [the legendary Hall of Fame coach at Winston-Salem State]. I thought I would end up going to N.C. A&T."

North Carolina also wanted McAdoo. He was an athletic standout at Ben L. Smith High in Greensboro—he and fellow Tar Heel Bobby Jones faced off not only in basketball but also at track meets in the high jump—but McAdoo barely missed academically qualifying for the school.

"I don't think the SATs were ever fair because they were culturally biased," former North Carolina coach Dean Smith said in our interview for this book. "But McAdoo could have qualified under present standards."

Ultimately, McAdoo decided to go to junior college at Vincennes, Indiana. In his first season at Vincennes, McAdoo averaged 19.3 points per game, and Vincennes won the national junior-college championship.

"I had originally planned on being in junior college for one year and then transferring to UCLA," McAdoo said. "I needed a 3.0 [grade point average] to transfer after one year. I ended up with a 2.9."

So McAdoo went back for his second year. He was having problems with his mail—apparently, some letters to Vincennes from then-UCLA assistant coach Denny Crum and coach John Wooden never got to him.

"Since I hadn't been hearing from UCLA, my interest went to Carolina all of a sudden," McAdoo said. "I saw they were only losing one player, Lee Dedmon, and I thought maybe I could just slide in there and take his place."

That's exactly what McAdoo did, which was fortunate for the Tar Heels since they had just lost a bitter recruiting battle with Maryland for Tom McMillen and needed another big man. Immediately.

"My junior college team was fantastic, although I didn't know that at the time," McAdoo said. "But that summer I went to try out for the Pan-Am Games, and out of about 75 guys I made a 12-man team. I just destroyed about half those guys. The team I turned out to have come from in Vincennes—it was better on a pure talent level than that North Carolina team. No one believes that, but it's true. Every last player was a high-school All-American. I know Carolina was the NCAA instead of junior college, but the ACC was actually a step back, talent-wise."

Recalled Smith: "I didn't believe in recruiting from the junior colleges, generally, because we believed in working your way up. If you bring in a junior, he might take away time from players who have been there a couple of years. But that was the year McMillen announced he was coming and then switched to Maryland. It was the perfect time for us. And Mac really went out of his way to be a part of the team from the beginning."

McAdoo averaged team highs of 19.5 points and 10.1 rebounds on the 1971-72 team. The UNC students started a proud chant that season that went: "We know what Dean can do, but what can Mc-A-Doo?" McAdoo could do about everything, but the team still lost in the national semifinals to Florida State. McAdoo scored 24 points and snared 15 rebounds in that game, but he fouled out early. The rest of the Tar Heels had bad shooting days—other than McAdoo, the team went a combined 19 for 51—and the Tar Heels lost, 79-75.

Said longtime Tar Heel radio voice Woody Durham, who called that game: "I thought McAdoo fouling out of the FSU game probably cost Carolina the game. McAdoo was really the missing link on that team—and I'm not even sure coach Smith really knew how good McAdoo was. He was one of the best shooters for a big man that I've ever seen."

The following season, McAdoo was rookie of the year with the Buffalo Braves (now the L.A. Clippers). By his third season, McAdoo was league MVP. He averaged more than 30 points a season three different times during his career and won two NBA championships, with the Lakers in 1982 and 1985. He was the sixth man on those Pat Riley-oached teams, and Riley was so impressed with him that he would later hire McAdoo as a Heat assistant.

At age 34, McAdoo went to Europe and played for six seasons in Italy.

"We won three Italian championships and a couple of European championships, and even though nobody talks about it, that was some of my very favorite time as a basketball player," McAdoo said.

Smith fondly recalls a phone call he received from McAdoo once while he was still playing in Italy.

"Can you send me the tape of the 1972 Final Four team?" McAdoo asked. "I've got to show it to these guys over here—they don't know how to play team basketball."

Toward the end of his time in Italy, McAdoo's wife was diagnosed with cancer. She came to the U.S. to be treated and lived for one more year. Her funeral was in Greensboro. Although McAdoo didn't tell the UNC Basketball office about the funeral, Smith showed up for it.

"I didn't even know he was paying attention," McAdoo said of his former coach, "but he heard about it somehow. I was out of the program and had been for many years. Him coming to the funeral—that meant a lot to me."

Now remarried, McAdoo's six children range in age from six to 32. He also has four grandchildren. And although he doesn't actively play basketball any longer, his shot is still sweet. He can—and still does—beat many members of the Heat in H-O-R-S-E.

BOB MCADOO BY THE NUMBERS

3	TIMES MCADOO LED NBA IN SCORING, EACH WITH A 30-PLUS POINT AVERAGE.
5	TIME NBA ALL-STAR.
10.1	REBOUNDING AVERAGE DURING ONE SEASON AT UNC.
19.5	SCORING AVERAGE DURING ONE SEASON AT UNC.
26-5	UNC'S RECORD DURING MCADOO'S ONE SEASON.

Where Have You Gone?

BOBBY JONES

Salt of the Earth

There is a simple verse in the Bible that most of us are familiar with. That verse now could serve as a headline above the life of Bobby Jones, the former North Carolina and NBA star who now helps lead a sports ministry.

The verse is Matthew 5:13. It begins: "You are the salt of the earth."

Said Jones as we sat together in the offices of "2XSalt" in Charlotte: "Salt heals. It flavors. It preserves. We want to be salt in this world."

At age 53, Jones has changed careers with the idea of changing more lives. From the late 1980s until 2004, he was a high-school basketball coach and administrator at Charlotte Christian. But he joined 2XSalt founder and former NBA player Bart Kofoed in May 2004, along with another basketball legend— former N.C. State player and Jones's close friend, David Thompson.

The ministry is youth-oriented, zeroing in on kids in middle and high school. "We're still feeling our way," Jones said. "At some point, we'd like to build our own facility and be able to work with kids around the clock. That's a vision down the road."

For now, the ministry will concentrate on activities like basketball and soccer camps, teaching kids about sports in a Christian setting. "We don't want conversion by concussion," Jones said. "We want to get to know the kids, let them know what we believe and let the Lord work through them."

Jones's own spiritual journey was flavored by many people, including his wife Tess and his former college coach, Dean Smith.

"Coach Smith knew I was exploring Christianity in college and he gave me a couple of books on it," Jones said. "He didn't really push it, he just said, 'You might want to look into this.' I really appreciated that."

UNC Athletic Communications

BOBBY JONES

1972-1974

Bobby Jones (above) averaged 13.7 points and 8.9 rebounds per game during his career at UNC. After 15 years as a basketball coach and athletic director at a private school in Charlotte, Jones (right) left that job in 2004 to join "2XSalt," a sports ministry based in Charlotte. That's former N.C. State star David Thompson that Jones is shooting over in the above photo. Thompson later became a great friend to Jones and is now also deeply involved in the "2XSalt" ministry.

When Bobby and Tess Jones were dating in college, Bobby wanted to get engaged during his senior year (1973-74). Said Tess: "I don't know if I can marry somebody if I don't know he is a committed Christian."

A committed Christian? What did that mean? Jones went to his parents' home in Charlotte to think about it some more. He had grown up going to church. But his perception then of Christians was that they were either weak people (which wouldn't work for him since he intended to play pro basketball) or missionaries (which he didn't want to do).

"But I got down on my knees and I realized that to be a committed Christian, you had to commit yourself completely to Jesus Christ," Jones said. "I had not done that. So I asked Jesus to forgive me of my sins and be my savior, but also to be the Lord of my life every single day."

For the past 30 years, Jones has tried to live by those principles. He and Tess have raised three children—Eric, Matthew, and Meredith—in Charlotte. And Jones has tried to teach thousands of kids on his teams and in his basketball camps that you can be a Christian and still be aggressive. In fact, he bemoans the fact that too many kids today are afraid to lose in competition.

"One thing youth these days don't do is they don't fail," Jones said. "And they don't succeed. They'll go to a gym and just shoot around. I tell kids they need to go play one on one. There needs to be a winner and a loser. That's how you get better. But I think a lot of kids don't want to be embarrassed."

Jones certainly failed some at UNC and in his 12-year career in the ABA and NBA, but he also had a startling amount of success. A 6-8, 215-pound forward, Jones is considered one of the finest defensive players ever at North Carolina.

"I could put him on David Thompson or Tommy Burleson," Dean Smith said in our interview for this book, "and he'd do a great job on either one."

Said Woody Durham, the radio voice of the Tar Heels since 1971: "If you had to draw up the qualifications of the ideal Carolina basketball player, Bobby Jones would be it."

Jones was always known for his team-first attitude. Before Jones ever got to North Carolina, Smith instituted the rule that players who scored a basket made sure on their way back down the floor to point at the man who made the assist. The players on the bench would point at the assist man in appreciation as well.

"Then, in Bobby's sophomore year, we started the Bobby Jones rule," Smith said with a laugh. "George Karl threw him a pass, he missed a pretty tough layup, and he comes back pointing at George anyway. We liked that so much we decided we wanted all of our guys to do that."

Former North Carolina star Billy Cunningham coached Jones in the NBA, and the two shared a title with the NBA-champion Philadelphia 76ers in 1983. Jones won the NBA Sixth Man Award for that squad.

"Bobby is one of the truly unique people I've ever met in my life," said Cunningham. "He's a caring, religious, loving man. He epitomized 'team.' As long as we won, he didn't care if he scored a single point. And never in the history of the NBA has anyone won more games on the defensive end of the court."

Jones was born in Ohio, but from sixth grade on he lived in Charlotte. The second of Bob and Hazel Jones's three children, Bobby had an older brother, Kirby, who preceded him at South Mecklenburg High and later played at Oklahoma.

Bobby Jones was gawky and somewhat uncoordinated as a high-school sophomore, but he matured into a star by the time he was a prep senior. He was also a high-jump standout, winning the state title twice and coming in second place once to Bob McAdoo.

Jones grew up shooting on a dirt court where most of the right side was washed away. Because of that, he was always more comfortable going to his left. Naturally left-handed, his father, Bob, switched him to righty when teaching his son the game. All that would come into play in Jones's senior year in 1974, when Jones stole an inbounds pass at Duke with the score tied at 71-all, hit a difficult left-handed layup at the buzzer, and kept right on running into the locker room.

The best UNC team Jones played on was his sophomore season in 1971-72, when McAdoo was still in Chapel Hill and the Tar Heels made the Final Four. Following that season, Jones—despite not being among the original 150 invitees—made the U.S. Olympic team, in large part because of his defensive prowess. He played on the U.S. squad many feel was cheated out of its rightful gold medal in Munich in 1972 when Russia had three chances to replay the game's final three seconds before scoring at the buzzer.

Jones and his teammates refused to accept the silver medal, leaving the medal stand empty on one side. Their medals still sit in a bank vault in Switzerland.

"I understood then that sports was just a business," Jones said. "And it wasn't the loss so much as the terrorists' massacre of the Israelis at those Olympics. When that happened all of us on the team thought, 'Well, surely the Olympics will be canceled.' Yet they weren't. But I'll say this—If I could do it again, I'd do it. It didn't turn out the way I wanted it to, but it was a great honor."

As a senior in 1974, both UNC-Duke games were memorable for Jones. The second was the famous eight-points-in-17-seconds comeback in Jones's final game at Carmichael Auditorium. Jones scored 24 points in that game—ultimately a 96-92 UNC win in overtime—and also had four points and a steal in those 17 seconds. He gives most of the credit for that victory to Dean Smith.

"He never showed any nervousness or apprehension," Jones said. "He always projected, 'Hey, we can do this.'"

The most difficult part of Jones's life, he said, came when he began having epilepsy attacks and heart problems as a pro player. He had his first seizure in college, but it was mis-diagnosed. He had more problems in Denver—first a heart arrhythmia and then more epileptic seizures. But with the help of Smith, who found a doctor at Duke for Jones to latch onto, Jones was able to get his health under control. Getting traded from Denver to Philadelphia in 1978 seemed to cure the heart arrhythmia; Jones figures the problem might have been the altitude. He began taking the drug phenobarbitol for the epilepsy and still takes it. He hasn't had a seizure in nearly 30 years.

Jones made the NBA's All-Defensive First Team for nine years in a row, and one of these years he may make it into the Basketball Hall of Fame (he's been a finalist). He still plays basketball occasionally himself, tries to be a good Christian and attempts to incorporate some of the lessons he learned at UNC.

"During my freshman year," remembered Jones, "Coach Smith brought me into his office and asked me, 'Bobby, are you the kind of player who needs to be yelled at in practice?' I was stunned he would ask me. I said, 'You know, Coach, I really don't like to be yelled at.' He said okay, and he never yelled at me once for four years."

Jones said he doesn't yell at any of his own players, either. It's not his nature. But he does recognize that each young person he tries to reach is unique.

"People are different and need to be treated differently," Jones said. "But everyone needs to be treated fairly. I learned that from Coach Smith."

BOBBY JONES BY THE NUMBERS

4   APPEARANCES IN NBA ALL-STAR GAME.

8   POINTS DOWN TO DUKE WITH 17 SECONDS TO PLAY IN 1974. JONES HELPED LEAD UNC'S COMEBACK TO WIN.

8.9   CAREER REBOUNDING AVERAGE AT UNC.

13.7   CAREER SCORING AVERAGE AT UNC.

21   REBOUNDS AGAINST DUKE AS A JUNIOR.

60.8   CAREER FIELD-GOAL PERCENTAGE AT UNC (JONES LED THE ACC IN THAT CATEGORY ALL THREE YEARS HE PLAYED).

Where Have You Gone?

MITCH KUPCHAK

I Love L.A.

Somewhere in Los Angeles, locked away in a safe-deposit box, eight NBA championship rings have been squirreled away by their owner. Mitch Kupchak, who earned all of them, doesn't like to wear rings. It's ironic, since he has enough to outfit an octopus, and many men spend their entire NBA careers in pursuit of just one. But Kupchak doesn't care much for the jewelry—he just likes what the jewelry represents. First as a player and now as the Los Angeles Lakers' general manager, Kupchak has been a grinder. He likes to win, and he knows what it takes to win, so he works his job with the relentlessness with which he once pursued rebounds in Chapel Hill.

Originally from New York, Kupchak has spent almost all of the past quarter-century in Los Angeles. He came there as a player in 1981, signing an unusual contract in which he agreed to work for the Lakers somewhere in the front office after his playing career ended. When it did due to injury problems, in 1986, Kupchak became the assistant general manager to the legendary Jerry West. He learned everything he could from West, and then, in 2000, became West's handpicked successor as Lakers GM when West moved on to the Memphis Grizzlies.

Since then, Kupchak has been all over the sports pages. He presided over the Shaquille O'Neal-Kobe Bryant feud and the letting go of coach Phil Jackson. In the summer of 2004, he tried to hire North Carolina coach Roy Williams and also Duke coach Mike Krzyzewski to replace Jackson.

"Make sure to note I offered the job to Roy first," Kupchak said in his interview for this book. "The Lakers have now had the distinct honor of being turned down by Roy Williams twice. We offered him the job eight or 10 years ago, when he was in Kansas, before we ever hired Phil Jackson. We got the same response then as we did this time."

MITCH KUPCHAK

1973-1976

Mitch Kupchak (above) was recruited from Long Island, New York, to play ball at North Carolina. He was named an All-American and the ACC Player of the Year during his senior season. Kupchak now has eight NBA championship rings, which he earned as both a player and a general manager. Here (right) he is with fellow Tar Heel Jackie Manuel at North Carolina's 2004 Lettermen's Reunion.

While Williams turned the job down flat, Krzyzewski listened intently to what Kupchak had to say before ultimately deciding to stay at Duke after a deliberation of several days. Kupchak ended up hiring Rudy Tomjanovich as the Lakers coach for 2004-05—part of a rebuilding of the franchise that won three consecutive NBA championships behind Shaq and Kobe from 2000-2002. Rudy T. quit midway through the season due to health problems, and so Kupchak had another issue to deal with. He ended up rehiring Jackson in June 2005, despite Jackson's oft-stated problems with Bryant. The move left some criticizing Kupchak and some praising his moxie.

That was nothing unusual. Kupchak came under fire for trading away O'Neal to Miami in 2004, once it became obvious that a choice between O'Neal and Bryant would have to be made. The two alpha-male superstars could barely stomach each other anymore. The Lakers, behind owner Dr. Jerry Buss and Kupchak, decided to attach their future to the much younger Bryant.

Kupchak was criticized for that in California, as some fans and reporters believed (probably naively) that West could somehow have kept Shaq and Kobe together. But the GM rolled with it. He still loves his job.

"How many people get to watch and scout games and talk basketball all the time, and get paid very well to do that?" he asked. "Plus, on top of that, for the L.A. Lakers? It's a dream."

Just a few weeks before he made the Shaq trade, Kupchak turned 50. Kupchak has a full head of gray hair now and an old knee injury that creeps up on him. More importantly, he has a wife (Claire), an eight-year-old son and a five-year-old daughter. He loves his family dearly. And they are all used to the constant presence of Kupchak's cellular phone in their lives as he tries to make the Lakers a little better each day. He takes pride in the team's high profile.

"At one time, this was a Dodgers town," Kupchak said of Los Angeles. "I think it's a Laker town now."

Growing up in Long Island, N.Y., in the 1960s, Kupchak probably would have had a hard time imagining a life on the West Coast. His father Harry worked for a construction company in Manhattan and helped build bridges. His mother Sonya took care of the four kids—Mitch has an older sister and two younger brothers. The family was of Ukrainian descent.

"My grandparents came over on the boat to Ellis Island in the 1920s," Kupchak said.

The Kupchaks lived in tract housing.

"There were blocks and blocks and rows and rows of houses that all looked basically the same," Kupchak said. "There must have been 60 or 70 kids in a two-block radius. You just opened the door in the morning and you were out. No playdates. No getting in the car. The drugstore and deli were down the block. There was always something to do—stickball, stoopball, baseball or basketball."

Kupchak's favorite sport as a kid was baseball, and his hero was Mickey Mantle. But when he grew to be six foot seven in junior high, a basketball coach saw him and persuaded him to start taking the sport seriously. Stan Kellner, that coach, remains a close friend of Kupchak's to this day.

"By 10th grade, I began to appreciate my height," said Kupchak, who eventually reached 6-10. "I was always a foot taller than most everyone. When you're young and you're different, that's not necessarily a good thing."

It became a good thing, though. Kupchak's success at enormous Brentwood High (enrollment: 5,000) led the Tar Heels to recruit him. Coach Dean Smith didn't promise Kupchak any playing time, and Kupchak actually liked that, because he knew Smith was telling the truth.

"I vividly remember Coach Smith telling me and my folks that he couldn't guarantee how much I'd play," Kupchak said. "Then he looked at my parents and said, 'I'll guarantee you he'll graduate. But the playing thing will depend on how hard he works.' That struck me. That set him apart from the rest."

Kupchak took his visit in the spring, before Chapel Hill had really heated up.

"The weather was gorgeous," he laughed. "I had no idea you could have one day after the next of 90 degrees with 90 percent humidity. I think I got tricked."

The NCAA allowed freshmen to be eligible before the 1972-73 season. Dean Smith has long opposed that rule and still does. But since it was in place, Smith made Kupchak the first freshman to ever play varsity basketball at North Carolina.

Kupchak enjoyed an outstanding career, averaging a double-double in his final two seasons. He was an All-American and the ACC Player of the Year as a senior in 1976, when he scored 17.6 points and grabbed 11.3 rebounds per game. He was known for his thoughtfulness, great work ethic, and high pain tolerance.

"Mitch was a double-double waiting to happen every time out," remembered Tar Heel announcer Woody Durham. "I sometimes wonder how good he could have been here had it not been for the injuries."

Said coach Dean Smith: "Mitch had to be one of the most courageous players we ever had here."

Once at Chapel Hill, Kupchak had to have back surgery. Smith showed up for the operation and watched it in his surgical scrubs—something Kupchak has always remembered.

"He's special to me," Smith said of Kupchak. "Of course, they all are."

Kupchak wishes he could have won more in Chapel Hill.

"I regret never advancing past the second round in the NCAAs," said Kupchak, one of the best Carolina players not to make a Final Four. "But I do appreciate becoming part of a family in Chapel Hill that has lasted for more than 30 years now, and I appreciate learning how to play basketball the right way. That overshadows any disappointment."

As a collegiate swan song, Kupchak made the U.S. Olympic team helmed by Smith in 1976, along with fellow Tar Heels Tommy LaGarde, Phil Ford, and Walter Davis. Kupchak was the starting center on the team that went to Montreal and avenged the controversial loss to the Russians in 1972—the one in which the U.S. team was robbed so badly by officials that Bobby Jones and his teammates didn't take their silver medals in protest.

"I probably made the 1976 team because my coach was the coach," Kupchak said modestly, "but that's okay. To win a gold medal, that clearly jumped out as a crowning moment."

Kupchak was drafted by the Washington Bullets, where he came off the bench for a veteran team led by Elvin Hayes and Wes Unseld that won the NBA championship in 1978. He was a toiler underneath the boards, facing off against men bigger than himself over and over. During his 10-season NBA career, he averaged a solid 10.2 points per game.

In 1981, Kupchak signed with the Lakers as a restricted free agent. The Bullets (now the Wizards) couldn't match the offer. So Kupchak, as a young man, went West. He has never looked back.

Always a fine student and a regular member of the Dean's List at UNC, Kupchak also enrolled in the MBA program at UCLA. He actually obtained that Master's degree while playing in the NBA. He's deeply rooted in California now, but he still comes back to Chapel Hill at least once a year and has signed a number of former Tar Heel players with the Lakers.

"I have a great take on what integrity is," Kupchak said. "I understand what it is to be a professional. I appreciate relationships with people. All that started at Carolina."

MITCH KUPCHAK BY THE NUMBERS

1   OLYMPIC GOLD MEDAL (1976, MONTREAL).

8   NUMBER OF NBA CHAMPIONSHIP RINGS.

8.5   CAREER REBOUNDS PER GAME AT UNC.

17.6   SCORING AVERAGE AS A SENIOR, WHEN HE WAS ACC PLAYER OF THE YEAR.

58.6   CAREER SHOOTING PERCENTAGE AT UNC.

1,006 CAREER REBOUNDS AT UNC (FIFTH ON ALL-TIME LIST).

1,611 CAREER POINTS AT UNC.

Where Have You Gone?

TOM LaGARDE

A Barn Full of Memories

The barn is huge. It sits outside Tom LaGarde's house on the seven acres he owns 20 miles outside Chapel Hill—serving both as a landmark and a reminder of times past.

"Just look for the white barn," LaGarde said when directing me to his house for our interview. "You can't miss it."

And you really can't. The barn used to house 50 cows. But the old milking stalls are now filled with fireplace mantels, cast-iron heaters and doors. There's also heart pine wood, bead board siding and hand-hewn wooden beams.

This is the storehouse for BarnStar Vintage Wood and Architectural Salvage, a company LaGarde and his wife, Heather, have started. They are capitalizing on the trend of homeowners who want their back porch made from wood salvaged from an old cotton mill built 100 years ago rather than from off the rack at Lowe's. The barn and its contents represent the latest chapter in LaGarde's adventurous life, which has wound back to the Chapel Hill area these days after more than 25 years away from the place he starred as a 6-10 forward/center in the mid-1970s.

LaGarde has a friend who has worked for hospice organizations and has counseled with many people who were close to dying. That friend once told him something that has stuck with him for years.

"The guy told me that people who were dying never regretted the things they did," LaGarde said. "They only regretted the things they didn't do. I always thought that was interesting. So I've tried a bunch of things in my life."

At age 50, Tom and Heather LaGarde have now settled into an old farmhouse built in 1932. It's a rambling, comfortable place, full of "to-do" projects that keep them both busy.

Tom has also started on parenthood late in life. He and Heather have two young children—five-year-old daughter Hadden and one-year-old son Holland.

TOM LaGARDE

1974-1977

Tom LaGarde (above) played a big part in the Tar Heels' success in 1977, scoring 15.1 points per game, until an injury to his knee in February ended his senior season early. Since his NBA career ended in 1984, LaGarde (right) has worked on Wall Street, served as commissioner of a Roller Basketball league, and today operates his own wood and architectural salvage company.

LaGarde named his son for Holland's great-grandfather, who emigrated from Holland in 1912. The LaGardes share their farmhouse with a dog and three cats.

Before moving into this pastoral setting, however, LaGarde worked on Wall Street, lived overseas, won an Olympic gold medal, and served as the commissioner of a New York basketball league where all the players wore inline skates.

"I think most people thought I was crazy, but I enjoyed it," said LaGarde of his days as the guru of "Roller Basketball."

More on that later. First, it's important to understand where LaGarde came from. In a number of ways, he was unique in his family. LaGarde grew up in Detroit, the son of Tom and Mary LaGarde, in what he describes as a "very blue-collar family." His father drove a bus for 38 years for the city of Detroit. No one in the family had been able to go to college before LaGarde.

LaGarde's height also made him unusual. Like all tall kids, he was encouraged to play basketball. He discovered he enjoyed it and starred at an all-boys Catholic high school in Detroit.

"I was pretty shy," LaGarde said. "All I did was play basketball and study."

North Carolina joined a cast of dozens of schools recruiting LaGarde. After a while, LaGarde noticed that most of the schools constantly used "negative recruitment" to try to downgrade their rivals in LaGarde's eyes, yet none of the coaches seemed to have a bad thing to say about Dean Smith.

That—along with the look of the campus and a visit where he got to interact with his future teammates rather than just the assistant coaches—sealed it for LaGarde. He entered Chapel Hill in 1973 but barely played as a freshman in Smith's senior-oriented system.

"I didn't understand basketball, I found out pretty quickly," LaGarde said. "I was just a big kid who could run and jump."

The rest of LaGarde's career at Chapel Hill was one of steady, occasionally spectacular progression until midway through his senior season. As a sophomore, LaGarde won a starting spot and averaged a modest 7.7 points per game. As a junior, he led the ACC in field-goal percentage at 61.2 percent. Following that season, LaGarde tried out for and made the U.S. Olympic team coached by Smith that won the gold medal in Montreal.

Then, as a senior in 1976-77, LaGarde was having his best season yet. Averaging 15.1 points and 7.4 rebounds per game, he was a standout on a team that also featured freshman Mike O'Koren and LaGarde's 1976 Olympic teammates, Walter Davis and Phil Ford.

"Coach Smith was fair, but there was no nonsense," LaGarde said. "He was well-respected by everybody, if not adored. It was really a tight ship, but a happy ship. We ran so much at the end of practice, we always knew we were in better shape than the other team. Coach was so prepared, and we were so ready, that it was fun to be in close games, because we knew we would win. It was a shock to lose—that's what I remember most about those years."

But in February 1977, LaGarde's senior season changed dramatically for the worse.

"We were in practice, doing some drill we normally didn't do—full-court one on one," LaGarde said. "I was going against Jeff Wolf. He was guarding me, and as I stopped to shoot a jump shot, he lost balance and he hit me. My knee straightened and just popped. And that was it."

LaGarde was lost for the rest of his senior season. Without him, the Tar Heels still managed to get all the way to the 1977 NCAA final, where they were beaten by Marquette.

With a healthy LaGarde, would UNC have won it all?

Said Tar Heels radio voice Woody Durham: "Tommy LaGarde had a tremendous work ethic. He really wanted to get better, and he did. If we had him in 1977, who knows?"

Even with the torn-up knee, LaGarde was a second-team All-America (he also made academic All-American twice in his career). And he was the No. 9 overall pick of the NBA draft, chosen by the Denver Nuggets. So began an up-and-down pro career, hampered by knee problems but also containing some nice moments. LaGarde didn't think his knee was ready his rookie year against Denver, but the Nuggets wanted him to play anyway, and he had a poor season.

Denver quickly traded him to Seattle for the 1978-79 season, where he was a starter averaging 11 points and nine rebounds for a very good team until his leg got stepped on while he was jumping for a dunk. That tore up his other knee. Seattle ended up winning the NBA championship that season, so LaGarde got a championship ring, although he played in only the first quarter of the season.

After one more year in Seattle, LaGarde was put on the expansion list, where the Dallas Mavericks picked him up and played him for two seasons. He went to Italy for a couple of seasons after that, becoming so fluent in the language that he actually started to dream in Italian. Then he came back for one game with the New Jersey Nets in 1984, got hurt once more, and never played professionally again.

Then LaGarde tried Wall Street. Tommy Kearns, a member of the 1957 North Carolina championship team, was helpful in getting LaGarde a job at Morgan Stanley, where he sold bonds. He enjoyed it for a while, but it "didn't seem like something I wanted to do for the rest of my life," LaGarde said.

He went to France for a year in 1990, and then came back to New York and got involved in inline skating.

"New York is just a big roller rink," LaGarde said. "And it was good for my knees. I could skate 30 miles, but I couldn't run one mile."

LaGarde still loved basketball, and wondered if the two sports could be married. He became commissioner of a fledgling "Roller Basketball" league that featured both adult and junior leagues.

Rollerblading was a national craze, and it seemed LaGarde might have caught a wave. Some ex-Wall Street people donated money to the league. Roller basketball caught on in Europe, where the world championship is still held every year. LaGarde and his friends experimented with the rules to make the game more exciting. Only man-to-man defense could be played. Each team had four skaters, not five. They not only had a three-point line, they also had a four-point line "which was great if you were down 12 with a minute to go," LaGarde said.

And you didn't have to take the ball out of bounds after a made basket in Roller Basketball—that way the players could zip up and downcourt more quickly. (LaGarde believes changing that rule would speed things up considerably in the NBA as well.)

"We got a lot of attention with me as an ex-basketball player," LaGarde said. "We got on CNN. But our exposure came too early. We hadn't developed the expertise. After four years, instead of three or four really good players, we had 30-40. But by then it was too late—the exposure had come and gone."

Once the dot-com bubble burst in the late 1990s, LaGarde's financiers dried up. He didn't have enough money to run the league himself—an early divorce had hurt him a bit financially.

"I had to close up shop," he said.

Heather LaGarde is from Chapel Hill, and the family decided to relocate nearby. The state has brought closer some of their happiest memories, as they raise their young family and fill their barn with vintage wood.

"A lot of the things about UNC you don't appreciate until you leave," LaGarde said, "because your life experience is so minimal. But once you do leave you realize that life can be messy. As far as basketball, UNC was the most perfect situation that I've ever been in."

TOM LAGARDE BY THE NUMBERS

1	OLYMPIC GOLD MEDAL (1976, MONTREAL).
2	TIMES NAMED ACADEMIC ALL-AMERICAN.
5.3	CAREER REBOUNDING AVERAGE PER GAME AT UNC.
15.1	POINTS PER GAME LAGARDE WAS AVERAGING DURING HIS SENIOR SEASON BEFORE HE TORE UP HIS KNEE.
58.3	CAREER FIELD-GOAL PERCENTAGE.
80.9	LAGARDE'S FREE-THROW PERCENTAGE AS A JUNIOR (SECOND IN THE ACC THAT SEASON).
1,007	LAGARDE'S TOTAL POINTS AT NORTH CAROLINA.

Where Have You Gone?

PHIL FORD

Not a Slam Dunk

He scored more points for North Carolina than Michael Jordan or James Worthy or Antawn Jamison or Vince Carter or Lennie Rosenbluth or Sam Perkins or any other player who ever pulled on a Carolina blue uniform.

Despite all that, Phil Ford couldn't dunk.

"Never did it in my life," Ford said. "Not in a game, anyway. I sort of half-dunked once at a pep rally in Rocky Mount. But since that's the only time I got up that high, I'm counting it."

Ford wasn't that fast, either.

"Especially not in a 100-yard dash," he said. "But in a five-yard dash, you'd have a hard time beating me."

What Ford was, though, was an absolutely incredible college basketball player. And perhaps no player is more associated with the Tar Heels than Ford. When the 6-2 point guard held four fingers up high with his left hand while dribbling with his right, the game was over. No one ran the "Four Corners" like Ford did, with the ball seemingly attached to an invisible string.

Ford, now 49, was one of the most important players in Dean Smith's career at North Carolina. Ford's parents were both public schoolteachers in Rocky Mount, and each earned master's degrees. His mother Mabel valued the idea of education more than she valued basketball. That showed the first time that Dean Smith came to the Fords' house to recruit her son.

"When Dean came to visit me," Ford recalled, "we didn't talk about basketball for the whole first hour. We talked about race relations and what it means to be a good student, and finally we got into basketball a little."

Eventually, Phil Sr. (whom everyone called "Big Phil"), Mabel, and Phil Jr., walked Coach Smith to his car and saw him pull away. Then Mabel Ford said to

UNC Athletic Communications

PHIL FORD

1975-1978

Phil Ford (above) was a three-time All-America selection at point guard and is No.1 on UNC's career scoring list with 2,290 points. In the summer of 2005, Ford (right) followed head coach Larry Brown from Detroit to New York, where Ford now serves as an assistant coach on Brown's staff with the New York Knicks. Here, Ford speaks at the 2004 UNC Lettermen's Reunion banquet.

Jeffrey Camarati/UNC Athletic Communications

her husband: "Big Phil, wasn't it nice for the University of North Carolina to send an actual dean of the college all the way down here to call on Little Phil?"

"Little Phil" became the national college player of the year as a senior in 1978 playing for that college "Dean." But life wasn't as easy after that. Ford battled alcoholism for years as an adult and had to go to alcohol rehab several times. Despite the public embarrassment that his addiction and his two arrests in the late 1990s for drunk driving caused, Ford considers himself a very lucky man.

"By the grace of God, I didn't kill anyone," Ford said. "I didn't kill myself. I didn't have to go to prison. It could have been a lot worse. It was a hard lesson, but I had to learn it."

Ford regularly attends Alcoholics Anonymous meetings and said he hopes that sobriety will never again lose its importance to him.

"I go to my meetings, I go to Bible studies on Wednesday nights, I go to Sunday school and to church," Ford said. "I'm trying. I'm in position to be a better coach than I've ever been in my life because of all the hardships I've gone through."

At one point, Ford was considered a possibility as the future North Carolina head basketball coach. He was an assistant coach under Smith and then Bill Guthridge from 1988-2000 in Chapel Hill. But in large part because of his alcohol problems, Ford wasn't a serious candidate for the job once Guthridge left. Instead, Matt Doherty was hired in 2000, and Ford was basically fired as an assistant. Doherty brought in an entirely new staff of assistants in a move that rankled many Tar Heel loyalists (and one Doherty now says he should have approached differently).

Ford didn't leave the university, though. He was quickly hired by the Rams Club, which is the university's athletic fundraising arm. Ford worked there for four years, raising money for his beloved university, going to a lot of banquets— he always drinks cranberry juice now—and doing a little bit of TV and radio announcing.

One habit Ford never could shake—he always refers to the Tar Heels as "we," as in "We really need a basket right here." That's a journalistic no-no but was an oddly endearing habit. Ford has loved the university so much for so long, that he simply couldn't change it.

"There has never been a guy more loyal to Carolina than Phil, I can tell you that," said Dean Smith in our interview for this book. "When Matt came in with his own group of coaches, Phil could have been very harmful to him. Instead, Phil was the first to help Matt whenever he needed it."

At the North Carolina lettermen's reunion in 2004, Ford was one of the six former players who spoke. He talked lovingly of his alma mater, with tears streaming down his face.

By the summer of 2004, Ford had turned down "seven to eight" coaching jobs, by his count. Then Ford accepted a job with Larry Brown, another former

North Carolina point guard who became one of basketball's premier coaches. Brown was just coming off an NBA championship season with the Detroit Pistons and wanted Ford to join his Tar Heel-laden staff as an assistant.

"I did it because Coach Brown is a great, great coach," Ford said. "He reminds me a lot of Coach Smith."

That career move made for an exciting 12 months. The Pistons came within an eyelash of winning their second straight NBA title, extending San Antonio deep into the fourth quarter of Game Seven in the NBA Finals before faltering. Ford greatly enjoyed coaching former UNC standout Rasheed Wallace—one of his favorite former Tar Heels—and would have stayed in Detroit for several years.

"It was a fantastic season," Ford said.

But Brown and the Detroit brass had some well-documented battles. Brown is a dragonfly genius of a coach—a Hall of Famer who flits from job to job every few years. Brown and the Pistons split up in the offseason, and almost immediately Brown was hired to coach the New York Knicks. The Knicks will be the eighth NBA team that Brown, 64, has coached.

Brown asked Ford to join him as an assistant coach with the Knicks, and Ford accepted. He, his wife Traci and their two children immediately started planning their move to New York.

Ford knows that the Knicks are in massive need of rebuilding and will constitute a major challenge.

"But I'm a glass-half-full kind of guy," Ford said. "I always believe you can come back from eight points down with 17 seconds left."

Ford's ultimate dream—once deferred but now resurrected—is to run his own basketball program somewhere.

"I want to be a head coach," Ford said. "Just about every assistant coach does. But I'm also very satisfied doing what I'm doing right now."

As a player, Ford made it to one Final Four. In 1977, as a junior, he led a team that lost in the finals to Al McGuire's Marquette squad. Many fans also still remember Ford's final regular-season game as a senior in 1978, when he scored a career-high 34 points against a Duke team featuring Mike Gminski, Jim Spanarkel, and Gene Banks in an 87-83 win. His number—12—is one of only seven retired jerseys in UNC basketball history.

As an assistant coach, Ford was part of six more North Carolina Final Four teams, including the NCAA championship squad of 1993.

"If you ask an honest ACC fan to pick the best five players ever in the league by position, every one of them should pick Phil as the point guard," Woody Durham concluded. "He just was. He protected the ball, made free throws, ran the Four Corners, and could score from anywhere in big games. But honestly, Phil was not that great of an outside shooter. What he did was sort of like what

Larry Miller seemed to do—it was like he willed the ball into the basket on his jumper."

Always, Ford was renowned for his toughness. One story, repeated countless times in Chapel Hill throughout the years, has become legendary.

"In the ACC tournament during my sophomore season [in 1976] we were playing Clemson," Ford said. "Stan Rome elbowed me in the mouth and knocked one of my teeth out. I kept my dribble alive, handed the tooth to the trainer, and kept on playing."

This so impressed Dean Smith that he used the story for years with the rest of his teams as an example of grace under pressure. J.R. Reid used to joke about how the story grew over the years when Ford was also in the Tar Heel locker room.

"Coach Smith," Reid would say, "could you tell us about the time that Coach Ford jumped on a bomb while he was on the court, got his arm blown off, kept his dribble alive, and kept on playing?"

Ford is asked often about his favorite memories as a player at Chapel Hill but said he doesn't have a particular one.

"My entire experience as a student-athlete at Carolina was just unbelievable," said Ford, whose 2,290 points for UNC leads No. 2 all-time scorer Sam Perkins by 145. "But I will say the older I get, the more winning a gold medal means. When you're a player, you just look at it as another tournament. But looking back on it, standing on that podium with the national anthem playing and a gold medal around your neck, that was pretty neat."

Ford got to experience that with Smith. Smith was the coach of the 1976 U.S. Olympic team, and Ford was one of the four Tar Heel players selected to play on that all-collegiate squad—Mitch Kupchak, Tommy LaGarde, and Walter Davis were the other three.

Ford did have a moderately successful pro career, becoming the NBA Rookie of the Year in 1979 for the Kansas City Kings. He had three straight very good seasons, averaging 15-17 points per game for the Kings, before an injury changed his basketball life in February 1981. That's when Ford took an accidental thumb to the eye while trying to defend a pass from World B. Free.

The injury was ironic—Free loved to shoot but hardly ever passed the ball. It was also quite serious. Even now, Ford occasionally has double vision in the eye. He was never the same player again. His career petered out after four more seasons.

Ford hasn't played any sort of basketball since 1991, not even a pickup game.

"It's a young man's sport," said Ford, who now bears a striking resemblance to Magic Johnson. "I've heard too many horror stories about old men playing basketball. I've finally got two good hips [he had his second hip replacement in April 2004], and I'm going to keep them."

The Ford family all turned out successfully. Phil's brother, Wayne Ford, is a dermatologist. Ford's sister Jackie followed in her parents' footsteps and became a schoolteacher.

And now Ford—although he turns 50 on February 9, 2006—would love to become a head coach. It won't be a slam dunk. But for Ford, that's never been a problem before.

PHIL FORD BY THE NUMBERS

3   TIME FIRST-TEAM ALL-AMERICAN.

4   CORNERS, WHICH FORD RAN BETTER THAN ANYONE ELSE.

12   FORD'S JERSEY NUMBER (RETIRED).

18.6   CAREER SCORING AVERAGE.

34   POINTS SCORED IN HIS LAST HOME GAME IN A WIN OVER DUKE.

52.7   CAREER FIELD-GOAL PERCENTAGE.

99-24   UNC'S OVERALL RECORD DURING FORD'S FOUR SEASONS.

2,290   CAREER POINTS AT UNC (UNC ALL-TIME RECORD).

MIKE O'KOREN

The 'Upper Lower Class'

W hen asked during his Chapel Hill days to describe his New Jersey background, Mike O'Koren declared, "I'm from the upper lower class."

It was a funny quote, and also an appropriate one. O'Koren had grown up in project housing in New Jersey, raised by a single mother after his father died when O'Koren was 12. But O'Koren was also proud of his family and always intent on moving up—toward the next rebound, the next jump shot, the next anything.

That quote is still relevant to O'Koren's life. Once a three-time All-American at North Carolina in the late 1970s, he is now a member of the coaching fraternity's "upper lower class." He gets paid a very good salary for being an NBA assistant coach with the Washington Wizards. But for all the attention O'Koren now gets, he may as well be in a witness protection program.

Like NFL offensive linemen, soccer fullbacks and cycling *domestiques*, NBA assistants are essential but often overlooked. The head coach is the front man, while the assistant coaches quietly do the scouting reports, break down the tape, and serve as liaison from head coach to players. O'Koren, 47, doesn't mind that shadows have followed the spotlight, however. He learned the team concept at North Carolina, he said, and he's quite satisfied with what he does now because of that.

"This is no picnic, what I do," O'Koren said. "As all coaches know, there's no such thing as a five-day work week. In the NBA, you can be on a red-eye flight coming home on Thanksgiving Day. You can play on Christmas Day. It's hard work. But it's very enjoyable."

A number of Dean Smith's former players have followed him into coaching, including George Karl, Larry Brown, Bob McAdoo, Buzz Peterson, Jeff Lebo,

UNC Athletic Communications

MIKE O'KOREN

1977-1980

Forward Mike O'Koren (above) was a three-time All-American who posted the following line in a game against Duke during his junior season: 20 rebounds, 17 points, seven assists and four steals. Today, O'Koren (right) is an assistant for the Washington Wizards, where one of his responsibilities is coaching former Tar Heels Antawn Jamison and Brendan Haywood.

Washington Wizards

Eddie Fogler, Phil Ford, and Billy Cunningham. But O'Koren didn't really mean to.

After O'Koren's solid but unspectacular eight-year NBA career ended in 1988, the New Jersey Nets thought enough of him that they hired him for the front office. O'Koren had played 392 of his 407 career NBA games with the Nets. They—like most everyone who meets O'Koren—were impressed with his candor, sense of humor, and basketball smarts. Mostly, O'Koren was the team's radio analyst. For about a decade, he held that job with the Nets, which also involved a number of community appearances. Occasionally, O'Koren would dabble in a bit of scouting as well.

But then the Nets fired head coach John Calipari and all of his assistants in March 1999. Interim coach Don Casey asked O'Koren to step out of the broadcast booth and join the coaching staff.

"First it was just going to be for a couple of games, but then it turned into the rest of the season," O'Koren said.

Said Dean Smith, whom O'Koren credits for his love of coaching: "I was totally surprised when he started coaching, but he's done marvelously well, and now he really loves it."

Casey became the full-time coach of the Nets later in 1999 and retained O'Koren as an assistant. O'Koren would ultimately stay with the Nets until the summer of 2003, when former Nets assistant Eddie Jordan got the head coaching job with the Washington Wizards. Jordan then brought O'Koren with him. O'Koren even subbed in for Jordan for a couple of games in 2004, going 1-1 while Jordan made a brief stay in the hospital due to a blood clot in his leg.

Wizards center Brendan Haywood—who, like Antawn Jamison and O'Koren, is a former Tar Heel turned Wizard—said O'Koren did well during his time in the head chair.

"Mike O'Koren isn't your average assistant coach," Haywood told *The Washington Post*. "He has a lot of confidence in himself and in his ability to coach this team. When he's in the huddle, it doesn't seem that he is an assistant. It seems like he's a natural head man. That's why we played well."

O'Koren is no stranger to playing well. Like Phil Ford, he was a star at Carolina from his freshman year onward. As a 6-7 freshman forward, O'Koren was a standout for the Tar Heels on the team that got all the way to the 1977 NCAA final before losing to Marquette. He scored 31 points in the national semifinal against UNLV, beating his man time and again for backdoor cuts on passes from Ford. When asked if 31 was his career high in points, O'Koren proclaimed, "So far!"

O'Koren would never score more than that for the Tar Heels, but he could fill up a stat sheet like nobody's business. In what he describes as his favorite all-time game as a UNC player, O'Koren had 20 rebounds, 17 points, seven assists, and four steals in a 74-68 victory over Duke his junior season. Not only that, but he also guarded Duke star Gene Banks in that game and held Banks scoreless in the second half.

"I'm not a big Duke fan, even now," O'Koren said.

O'Koren was known as a free spirit at UNC whose feelings were always etched across his face.

"I was never one to let the truth get in the way of a good story," O'Koren said.

"He was a hard, hard worker and a really funny guy," said Woody Durham, the longtime radio voice of the Tar Heels. "And if he'd had a Bobby Jones or a Sam Perkins or an Eric Montross in the middle, I think we would still be talking about all the things those teams did at Chapel Hill."

O'Koren is married, and he and his wife, Angela, have one daughter, Chelsea.

"These days," O'Koren said, "I'm really a pretty boring guy unless you get me to go out with you."

O'Koren was in Chapel Hill not long ago and was able to catch up with his old coach, Dean Smith, for lunch. "I had so many laughs in that hour," Smith said.

Said O'Koren: "That was one of the best lunches of my life."

But then it was back to work. O'Koren had more things to do in his life as an unsung assistant coach.

Smith certainly understood.

MIKE O'KOREN BY THE NUMBERS

2   TIMES O'KOREN LED THE TAR HEELS IN ASSISTS (AS A FORWARD).

3   TIME ALL-AMERICAN.

8   SEASONS IN NBA.

15.1   CAREER SCORING AVERAGE.

20   CAREER HIGH IN REBOUNDS (AGAINST DUKE).

31   BOTH O'KOREN'S JERSEY NUMBER AND HIS CAREER HIGH IN POINTS.

1,765   CAREER POINTS AT UNC.

MIKE PEPPER

Brushing Against Death

Mike Pepper had shot thousands of free throws in his life. As he lined up for this one on December 17, 2003, at a high-school gym in Virginia, he had no idea it would be the most significant. At age 45, more than 20 years removed from the days when he shot free throws at North Carolina, Pepper was merely participating in a common pickup basketball ritual. He had to make this free throw to get to play in the next game.

He squared up to the basket. He bounced the ball once. Twice. Three times. He bent at the knees, then straightened up and let fly. As the ball sailed through the air, toward the basket 15 feet away, something terrible was happening inside Pepper's brain.

"Literally during the motion of the free throw, I had this very uneasy, awkward feeling," Pepper said. "It was like a very slow brain rush, from the front of my head to the back of my head."

The free throw swished. Pepper—who had maintained his college playing weight of 188 and had played pickup basketball regularly all his life—was in for the next game. But suddenly, he didn't feel like playing.

"Guys," Pepper said, "I'm going to sit this one out. Just give me a few minutes."

Pepper walked slowly to the side of the court and sat there for 15-20 minutes, his headache steadily worsening.

"This isn't going away," Pepper said to himself.

But that was no problem, really, was it? Pepper was tough. Like a number of healthy men in their 30s and 40s, he hadn't been to the doctor in years. Didn't even have a doctor, actually. He probably hadn't had a real physical since his days at Chapel Hill, when he was a starter for the 1981 team that made it all the way to the national final before losing to Indiana.

MIKE PEPPER

1978-1981

Mike Pepper (above) averaged 6.1 points per game as a starter on UNC's 1981 Final Four team. The fact that Pepper is doing anything nowadays is remarkable. In late 2003, he survived— and has since fully recovered from—a cerebral aneurysm that put him in a coma for eight days. Here (right) he is with his kids, Sara and Dane.

Pepper decided he would go home, pop an Advil or two, and gut it out. He had a full week ahead of him: coaching his son's basketball games; going to an important meeting at his commercial real-estate office; driving five hours from northern Virginia to Fayetteville, North Carolina, to see his girlfriend and go to a Christmas party. Being sick was going to be a major inconvenience. So Pepper decided he just wouldn't *be* sick.

"I was going to muscle my way through it," Pepper said.

For four days, he did. Even though he sat on the edge of his bed one night for more than an hour, wondering what was wrong. Finally, after he kept complaining about his headache, one of his friends pulled Pepper aside.

"You've got to get yourself checked out," Joe Robinson said.

Pepper did. He didn't know where to go or whom to call, so he ended up at an urgent-care center. He took a number and waited. Only when the doctor heard Pepper tell him that he was experiencing the worst headache of his life did things start to happen quickly.

"Pick a hospital—Reston or Fairfax," the doctor said. "You're going in!"

Pepper went to the emergency room, where they did a CT scan of his head. It was normal. But the doctors also did a spinal tap.

"And that was what probably saved Mike Pepper's life," said Dr. Mark Vasiliadis, now Pepper's family physician.

If all was okay with the spinal tap, the fluid drawn out of Pepper should have been clear. Instead, it was blood-red. Pepper had a cerebral aneurysm. He was fortunate he wasn't dead already. Although the aneurysm was leaking blood, it hadn't burst. But he had to have surgery immediately. An ambulance pulled up so Pepper could switch hospitals—the one in Fairfax was better equipped to deal with his case than the one he had chosen, in Reston.

Once he got there, doctors performed what would be the first of three delicate surgeries on Pepper's brain. They went inside Pepper's skull, clipped the aneurysm at the base of his brain and closed his skull. By this time, Pepper's family had mobilized. His two children were with their mother. His six sisters— Pepper is the only boy in a family of seven—were trying to take care of things. But Pepper wasn't finished with his medical odyssey. Three days after the operation, he started developing post-operative complications. His brain was swelling badly due to post-op trauma.

A flap of Pepper's skull had to be removed to release some of the pressure. Doctors put it in what was basically a refrigerator, hoping to put it back at some point. By now, Pepper was in a coma, where he would stay for eight days. At that point, it was quite possible Pepper would die. And if he did survive, the neurological damage could be so severe that he might never be able to totally function on his own again.

But, slowly, Pepper came out of the coma and back into the world. The North Carolina basketball family started offering all the support it could.

Pepper's old coaches called. The basketball secretaries called. Woody Durham called.

"There was an incredible outpouring from the Carolina family," Pepper said. "I received so many phone calls, letters, cards—many of them from people I had never even met.'

For 40 days, Pepper was in the hospital. He had to undergo a third surgery, where the part of his skull that was in the refrigerator was re-inserted like a piece of a puzzle.

When Pepper got out of the hospital, his head was still heavily bandaged. The Carolina lettermen's basketball reunion was only a couple of weeks away. Pepper decided he would go.

"I stuck out like a sore thumb because of the bandages," Pepper said.

But he went—a friend drove him—and the reunion helped him heal. Pepper received a standing ovation during the banquet after Durham, Carolina's radio play-by-play voice, described his situation at the microphone and pointed out that Pepper had still made it.

Said former Tar Heel coach Bill Guthridge, who saw Pepper that weekend in February 2004: "It's just unbelievable what he's been through. That was so touching that he came back for the reunion. For a while, it didn't look like he was going to live."

Instead, Pepper has made an unlikely and full recovery. Now 47, he can and does play full-court basketball again. His commercial real-estate business is thriving. He still maintains primary custody of his two children—Sara, 14, and Dane, 12. Dane's name is a variation on coach Smith's first name. "It's a sneaky way to get Dean into the family," Pepper laughed.

As for Pepper's recovery, everyone agrees it's been amazing. "He's 99.9 percent back," Dr. Vasiliadis said. "Most people in his situation would have died. But his fitness level, his fight and determination all really helped him."

Said Pepper: "You can't go through something like that without it affecting your life. There's no question I once took a lot of things for granted. That will never be the case again. I'm so thankful the good Lord looked after me, and that I have the opportunity to be in my kids' lives."

Pepper was a success story on the basketball court as well, during his days at Carolina. He was a late bloomer—on his first day of ninth grade in Flint Hill (Virginia), he was five feet tall and weighed less than 100 pounds. Pepper grew, and he was fortunate to be tutored by high school coach Stuart Vetter, who would eventually become a legend in his own field.

But Pepper was still lightly recruited in high school out of Virginia as a 6-3 guard. He thought his best offer was going to be playing at Appalachian State for Bobby Cremins. But he got in a postseason all-star game—a preliminary to the McDonald's all-star game—and happened to play the game of his life.

"Within a week, I had 40 or 50 offers," Pepper said. "Most were from mid-level Division I schools."

Guthridge contacted Pepper as well, saying he wasn't sure the Tar Heels had a scholarship available, but they were interested.

"This was the spring of 1977," Pepper said. "Carolina had just come back from playing in the national championship game [losing to Marquette], and Chapel Hill was abuzz. I was hanging out on my visit with all these guys I'd seen on TV all year. It was unbelievable. They sent me back home without a scholarship offer. But when Darnell Valentine, the No.1 point guard in the country that year, chose Kansas over North Carolina, he left an opening. I got it."

Pepper barely played early in his career. But by his junior year, he was a key reserve. And as a senior—on a team that Al Wood carried to the national final with an amazing 39-point game against Ralph Sampson-led Virginia in the Final Four—Pepper started every game and was a co-captain. Pepper's best individual moment came against Wake Forest in the ACC tournament semifinals, when he hit a 20-foot jumper with eight seconds to play to give North Carolina a 58-57 win.

Following college, Pepper was drafted by the then-San Diego Clippers in the sixth round, but it became clear to him that he wasn't good enough for the NBA.

"I was completely direction-less," Pepper said, "and then I just sort of fell into the commercial real-estate world."

Pepper has done that for close to 20 years. He works in northern Virginia for the world's largest brokerage firm—CB Richard Ellis—as a commercial real-estate broker.

But mostly, he spends his time just glad to be alive.

MIKE PEPPER BY THE NUMBERS

5   CAREER HIGH IN ASSISTS, VS. ST. JOSEPH'S AS A SENIOR.

6.1   SCORING AVERAGE AS A SENIOR, WHEN HE STARTED FOR UNC'S 1981 FINAL FOUR TEAM.

8   DAYS SPENT IN A COMA AFTER HIS CEREBRAL ANEURYSM IN LATE 2003.

14   CAREER HIGH IN POINTS, AGAINST VIRGINIA AS A SENIOR.

51.6   CAREER SHOOTING PERCENTAGE.

75.9   CAREER FREE THROW PERCENTAGE.

335   CAREER POINTS SCORED AT UNC.

AL WOOD

Meant to Be a Blessing

Al Wood slid into the restaurant booth smoothly. At age 47, his grace hasn't
evaporated. He's still a natural, whether standing behind a pulpit or in
front of a basketball team. Once, he did everything smoothly as a player, too.

"Of all the UNC players I've seen," said Woody Durham, the Tar Heels'
radio play-by-play announcer since 1971, "Al Wood was the very best shooter.
If I were going to pick two others, I'd put Jeff Lebo at No. 2 and Kenny Smith
at No. 3. But Al Wood has to be No.1—his shot was so pure."

But underneath that smooth surface, battles have raged. The most notable
one was the fight for Al Wood's soul.

The good side won that fight. In November 2004, Wood took a new job as
an associate pastor for MorningStar Ministries. The ministry is located at the old
Heritage USA site in Fort Mill, South Carolina, that was once the headquarters
of Jim and Tammy Faye Bakker's ministry before it went down in disgrace. Jim
Bakker has said in interviews that he believes MorningStar will "restore" the site
to its rightful glory. Wood, working under MorningStar founders Rick and Julie
Joyner, is a part of that process.

MorningStar also runs a school with about 125 students. Wood—who has a
wife and four children—is the headmaster and the coach of both the boys' and
girls' basketball teams.

"We want special students, those who are really on fire for the Lord," Wood
said. "We really want to push and prepare them for some type of ministry."

Besides his duties as a coach, Wood does a lot of public speaking and
preaching now. MorningStar has several churches in North Carolina. On most
Sundays, Wood speaks at one of them. The man who once scored 39 points in

AL WOOD

1978-1981

Two-time All-American Al Wood (above) missed zero games during his four-year North Carolina career, averaging 16.0 points per game. Here, Wood (right) speaks at the 2004 UNC Letterman's Reunion banquet. As a rapt audience watched, Wood talked eloquently about his love for Dean Smith and his personal struggles.

a 1981 Final Four game against Virginia, carrying UNC to victory over Ralph Sampson, also frequently talks to Fellowship of Christian Athlete groups.

"The most gratifying thing is that God has been able to put something in me that allows people to be moved when I speak about God's love," Wood said.

Wood also frequently shares his own testimony. It's a powerful story of a man whose father wasn't around and whose mother was an alcoholic who spent years in prison because she once killed her common-law husband in an alcohol-fueled rage. Years later, Wood would become an alcoholic himself.

"I always had great willpower," Wood said, sipping a cup of coffee. "My sophomore year at UNC, I wanted to do the mile run that we always had to do in less than five minutes. And I did it. I always could do things like that. But for some reason, it got to the point where if I was thinking about taking a drink, and I really didn't want to do it—I did it anyway."

Wood was a drinker during his six-year NBA career, but said the problem got far worse when his decent NBA career finished in 1986. He had money, plenty of free time, and no real purpose in life. His life started spiraling downhill. He began gambling as well.

"A couple of drinks lead to more and more, and you start doing some very erratic things," Wood said. "Alcohol affects your thinking. Everything escalates, and you've got problems."

In 1989, Wood realized his lifestyle was destructive. He and his wife, Robin, had two children and a third on the way. Wood started studying the Bible and also took some community-college classes on substance abuse to better understand the hold that alcohol had on his life.

"My daughter Candace was born in October 1989," Wood said, "and she hasn't even seen alcohol in my house."

Since that time, Wood has dedicated most of his life to church and family. His family has stayed in the Charlotte area since that's where Robin grew up. Wood grew up in Gray, Georgia, a small town of about 1,800 people that is 100 miles from Atlanta. It was a difficult childhood.

"I was around people who drank pretty much every weekend," Wood said. "It seemed like fun to them, and I thought that was the norm. That was my early childhood."

Wood's home situation was unstable enough that his grandmother adopted him. But he still saw his mother often, and he still remembers the night she had to go to prison. The county coroner came to his grandmother's house and rapped softly on the grandmother's window at 4 a.m., trying not to wake everyone up. Wood heard the knocking anyway and rose.

The coroner told Wood and his grandmother: "She killed him." They knew immediately what it meant.

"There was this guy my mother was living with," Wood explained as we sat in the restaurant. "It was basically a common-law marriage, I guess—she'd been with him for 15 years or better. One night they both were drunk, got into a fight, and she stabbed him. Then she had a blackout, and she didn't even realize it the next day. My mom died January 12, 2004, and it was something she had to live with the rest of her life. It really tormented her, because she had no intention of killing him."

Basketball got Wood out of Gray. He was a high-school star, but North Carolina wasn't one of the schools that contacted him through his high-school junior year. Impressed by the fact that Tar Heel players and coaches dominated the 1976 U.S. Olympic Team, Wood asked his high-school coach to write Dean Smith a letter.

"I initiated the contact," Wood said.

The Tar Heels took the bait, sending assistant coach Eddie Fogler to Wood's first game as a high school senior. Wood scored 58 points.

The Tar Heels were hooked, as was Wood. At 6-6, with fine driving ability to complement his feathery jump shot, Wood was quickly a star. He also bought into Dean Smith's system so thoroughly that he became deathly afraid of being late to anything, since that was one of Smith's firmest rules.

Once, when Wood had a flat tire on the way to a pregame meal, Wood simply left the car and hitchhiked to beat the clock. As a rookie in the NBA, he would later do the same thing in a rare Atlanta snowstorm to get to a home game—only to find out that the game was postponed, and he was the one player in the entire arena.

In Wood's final three seasons at UNC, he never averaged less than 17.8 points per game. A number of ACC observers believe Wood might have had the sweetest jump shot ever in the ACC. Wood doesn't think so—he would vote for Walter Davis from 15 to18 feet and J.J. Redick from three-point range.

"J.J. Redick is the best I've ever laid eyes on from 22 feet," Wood said. "I love watching him shoot, and I could care less if he's from Duke."

In one of the final games of his senior year, Wood said, the authorities arranged for his mother to get a temporary pass from prison so that she could come watch one of his games.

"Coach Smith recently sent me some highlight tapes on DVD from my senior season, and there was my mother sitting on the sideline," Wood said softly. "It was real nice to have her there."

Wood saved his best during that senior season, leading UNC to the national final with a thrilling 39-point performance against Virginia and Sampson. On Franklin Street in Chapel Hill, the phrase "Al Wood 39" was painted all over the asphalt with Carolina blue paint that evening.

Was Wood ever hotter than that in his career?

"No," Wood said. "And I thank God for Roy Williams being on the sideline that night [as an assistant coach]. Roy had seen me when I got into a zone in pickup games and couldn't miss. That game, for me, turned into a pickup game.

I completely went away from the norm of what we always did—the number of passes we made and all that. But after I'd shot about five in a row, Roy pretty much grabbed Coach Smith by the arm when he was about to pull me out and said, 'Aww, leave him alone.'"

Smith did, and Wood had his signature performance. The two had a close player-coach relationship.

Said Wood of Smith: "He's such a super individual that at his funeral one day, they could talk about him and never mention basketball. And people who didn't know him would think he was one of the greatest individuals who had ever lived."

Once, when Wood had a problem in college, Smith introduced his player to The Serenity Prayer: "God grant me the serenity to accept the things I cannot change, the courage to change the things I can, and the wisdom to know the difference."

Many years later, Wood would call Smith when he was ready to deal with his alcoholism. As Wood told the story publicly at the UNC Letterman Reunion in 2004: "Coach Smith didn't belittle me or put me down. He told me how much he loved me, and how much he appreciated me giving him a call."

Smith got Wood some help, and Wood has tried to return the favor in his own life. Although his wife, Robin, has had some health problems, and Wood has four busy children of his own—daughters Candace and Martina have both been high-school basketball standouts—Wood does a great deal of volunteer work in the Charlotte area.

"I was not blessed to keep it to myself," Wood said. "I was meant to be a blessing to someone else."

AL WOOD BY THE NUMBERS

0   GAMES MISSED IN FOUR-YEAR UNC CAREER.

2   TIMES AN ALL-AMERICAN.

16.0   CAREER SCORING AVERAGE.

39   POINTS AGAINST VIRGINIA IN THE 1981 FINAL FOUR.

56.0   CAREER FIELD-GOAL PERCENTAGE.

2,015   CAREER POINTS (FOURTH ON UNC'S ALL-TIME LIST BEHIND PHIL FORD, SAM PERKINS, AND LENNIE ROSENBLUTH).

Where Have You Gone?

CLIFF MORRIS

From MJ to M.D.

The business card of cardiologist Cliff Morris contains all the usual relevant information, plus the following quote: "Not all doctors are the same." Once you talk to Morris awhile, you understand this is true.

He is a doctor who doesn't want to just give you a pill and tell you to go away and get better. He wants to change your lifestyle and encourage you to find a passion that will make you healthier.

"One of the biggest problems with people who have a heart attack or stroke is depression," Morris said. "They used to be immortal in their own minds. Now they are mortal. So I do a stress test and an echocardiogram—I'll take care of you from beginning to end if you have a heart attack. But then I try to deal a lot with psychological issues. I spend a lot of time being a coach. I want to try and get people to link back to their passion—the things that not only make them happy, but also that give them life and make them breathe."

Morris, 42, practices medicine in the Richmond, Virginia, area. He once used to practice against Michael Jordan on a daily basis for the Tar Heels. Morris walked onto the JV team at UNC, made it, started getting some varsity practice time and eventually earned a scholarship, because his work habits were so impressive.

"I spent an awful lot of time guarding Jordan," Morris said, laughing. "And I take absolutely all the credit for everything Mike Jordan has done."

That's what people called Jordan back then, you know—Mike. In Jordan's first year as a Tar Heel, it was listed that way in the team media guide and on team posters before His Airness decided on the more melodious "Michael Jordan."

In practice, Jordan played furiously.

"Jordan would show no mercy against Cliff," said Bill Guthridge, who coached the Tar Heels from 1967-2000 as either an assistant or head coach.

126

CLIFF
MORRIS

1984-1985

Cliff Morris (above) only made it into 25 games at North Carolina, but he still calls his time on the basketball court "invaluable." Today, Morris (right) enjoys spending time with his wife, Fran. He is now a cardiologist in Virginia whose business card reads: "Not all doctors are the same."

"Jordan was an unbelievable competitor, and that was one of the reasons why he was so good. But Cliff would try so hard. He was a really good ingredient for us—one of those great practice players we've had through the years who used to be walk-ons and who were just thrilled to be on the team. You have to have guys like that."

Morris was one of those. He remembers that his finest moment as a Tar Heel basketball player actually came the day Dean Smith called him in Chapel Hill and told him he had won a varsity scholarship.

"Did you hear me screaming that day?" Morris said. "Half the world must have."

Morris got into only 25 varsity games in his career and scored just 15 points. Yet he believes his time on the basketball court at Chapel Hill was invaluable.

"One of the things I really drew from the UNC basketball experience was how to be a role player in life," Morris said. "You have to do your absolute best in your role. Even if I didn't get into the game, my contribution was getting the other guys ready to play, and I took pride in that. Now I'm in a group of about 30 cardiologists, and we also have to work together as a team. We service about six separate hospitals, and we're on call for each other's patients."

Missouri A. Morris, Cliff's mother, was a superb college player in her day. She had her basketball number retired at Hillside High in Durham, where she eventually became a teacher and an assistant principal. She raised Cliff and his two older sisters alone in Durham, N.C., after his father, who was in the Air Force, died in a plane crash. Cliff was two years old at the time.

Said Dean Smith: "Cliff's mother was great. She won teacher of the year honors several times. She did such a good job with him. He was so gung ho as a practice player for us, and now he's such a success as a cardiologist. I'm very proud of him."

Cliff excelled in academics and athletics in high school, but he knew his future wouldn't be basketball.

"Originally, in college, I wanted to be a marine biologist and live in an underwater house," he said. "But once I got into marine biology more, I decided I didn't want to do research the rest of my life. So I started thinking about Med School."

Morris graduated from medical school at UNC, then went to Richmond to do an internship and residency at the Medical College of Virginia. Along the way, he decided he wanted to specialize in cardiology because, he said: "I could read forever about the heart and all it does."

Morris also believes strongly in the power of the mind. He tries to keep morale in his office up with positive thinking and frequent high-fives with colleagues. Once, when he was on a business trip, Morris faxed back a picture of his hand with the word "energy" written in the middle. His colleagues taped it on the wall and would give the ghost "energy" hand an occasional high-five.

"I like to think of myself as a changer of perception," Morris said. "I want to change the perception of a heart attack for my patients. Don't think of it as the start of your demise. Think of it as something that is going to turn around your life."

Morris likes to tell his patients the story about the man who lay on his deathbed, smiled wearily and said: "I've been through an awful lot in my lifetime—most of which never happened." Most of his patients laugh, then nod—they understand the anxious times we live in.

Said Morris: "There is a lot of chaos in people's lives. You have to fight that. You have to fight anxiety. You have to position your own antennae so that the static goes away. There's not a pill in the world I can give them if their mind is enslaved by chaos."

Morris has four children, ranging in age from nine to 22. He and his second wife, Fran, have been married two and a half years.

"She's wonderful—a great soulmate and a great friend," Morris said.

Morris tries to keep in shape himself, figuring he should set a good example for his patients. He jogs every night with his chocolate Labrador retriever, Chico. In addition, he weight trains and sits on the advisory board of *Muscle & Fitness* magazine.

He also still thinks about those Tar Heel practices.

"Coach Smith always had a 'Thought of the Day' on the practice plan," Morris said. "You had to memorize it. If you didn't know it, you had to watch while the other guys ran. The saying was always something philosophical, and I loved those. That's kind of what I'm trying to do here. Take something philosophical, something deep, and then apply it to your fitness so you can get healthy."

CLIFF MORRIS BY THE NUMBERS

0.6   CAREER SCORING AVERAGE.

2   FORMER UNC BASKETBALL PLAYERS FROM THE 1980S WHO LATER BECAME MEDICAL DOCTORS (STEVE HALE IS A DOCTOR IN VERMONT).

5-FOR-11 MORRIS'S CAREER SHOOTING TOTALS AT UNC FOR BOTH FREE THROWS AND FIELD GOALS.

15   CAREER POINTS SCORED.

25   GAMES PLAYED AT UNC.

30   CARDIOLOGISTS IN MORRIS'S GROUP WHO WORK TOGETHER TO SERVE PATIENTS IN THE RICHMOND, VIRGINIA, AREA.

DAVE POPSON

Taking No Prisoners

Dave Popson spends many of his days behind bars, totally closed off from the outside world. He's not in jail himself. He works there.

Popson is a correctional activities specialist at a medium-security, all-male prison in Pennsylvania called SCI Retreat. Since 1999, he has run all sorts of activities for the 850 inmates there, including basketball, flag-football, soccer, and shuffleboard leagues. He also teaches a health and wellness class to the inmates.

"We teach them about nutrition, how to balance a checkbook—things that a lot of them have never encountered," Popson said. "Most of them actually are glad you're there, keeping them active. If we weren't there, they'd just be sitting in their cells, doing nothing."

What do you think would be the most popular sport in an all-male prison? According to Popson, it's weightlifting.

"Everybody lifts weights," Popson said. "Everybody wants to be big and bad."

It's a testosterone-heavy environment. Occasionally someone will challenge Popson, figuring they can make themselves look big by taking on the former North Carolina and NBA player.

Popson enjoys his work, but said it can wear on him if he isn't careful.

"After eight hours, you have to leave it all behind," Popson said. "It has to stay inside the gate. I always have to remember that this is my job, but this is not who I am. Then I take a long, slow drive, get my mind right, and go back to my family."

Popson, a six-foot-10 big man who averaged a modest 5.7 points per game, played basketball for the Tar Heels from 1983-87. He never got to participate in

DAVE POPSON

1984-1987

Dave Popson (above) averaged 10 points per game during his senior season in 1986-87, as the Tar Heels went 14-0 in the ACC. The Popsons (right)—Dave, his wife, Holly, and their daughter, Bella—now live in Pennsylvania. Dave works as a correctional activities specialist in an all-male prison for the state's Department of Corrections.

a Final Four, but he did play one year alongside Michael Jordan, when Jordan was a junior and Popson a freshman.

"He was an awesome player, but his competitive spirit was the most striking thing about him," Popson said. "Pool, cards, anything—he hated to lose. And he was tough on freshmen. But that was good, that's what you wanted. When we were seniors, we were rough on freshmen, too."

Popson grew up in Pennsylvania, the son of a coach. His father, Bernard, was a football coach and athletic director at Bishop O'Reilly, a private Catholic school in Kingston, Pennsylvania, for more than 30 years.

Bernard Popson was only 5-11, and his wife Mary Jo was 5-7. "I'm the only tall one in the family," Popson said. "My father saw that and said, 'Son, you're going to play basketball.'"

The Tar Heels took an interest in Popson during his junior season. "I remember to this day getting my first letter from Coach Smith, wanting to recruit me," Popson said. "That was a neat feeling."

Popson also visited Notre Dame, Virginia, and Kentucky, but he could tell basketball fever seemed most intense in Chapel Hill. The first team he played on was actually the best, Popson said; in his freshman season the Tar Heels started 21-0. That 1983-84 squad had Jordan, Sam Perkins, Kenny Smith, Brad Daugherty, and Matt Doherty on the same team. But Smith, the starting point guard, broke his wrist, and the team was never the same after that. The Tar Heels finished the regular season ranked No.1, but ended up getting upset in the second round of the NCAA tournament by Indiana.

Both that team and the one in Popson's senior year—1986-87—swept through the ACC regular season with perfect 14-0 marks. Oddly, though, neither of those teams won the ACC tournament nor made the Final Four. The loss in the 1987 NCAA tournament to Syracuse in the Elite Eight was the most difficult one to swallow, Popson said.

By his senior year, "Pop" was a fairly consistent scorer with a jump hook he could hit with either hand. He also sprinted quickly upcourt on fast breaks.

"I thought Dave could get up and down the floor about as well as any big man I'd ever seen," said longtime Tar Heels radio announcer Woody Durham.

Popson's greatest individual moment probably came against Maryland during his sophomore season. Under defensive pressure, Popson knocked in a 19-foot jumper from just outside the free-throw line with seven seconds left for the winning points in a 75-74 victory.

"The crowd absolutely exploded," Popson said.

Following his college career, Popson kicked around the NBA and the overseas leagues for five years, continuing to play basketball. He played in a total of 41 NBA games for four different teams, scoring 76 points. He also played in Monaco, Spain, and the CBA.

Among his most notable memories: Teaming with Larry Bird with the Boston Celtics toward the end of Bird's career, and watching Darryl (Chocolate Thunder) Dawkins devour an entire bucket of Kentucky Fried Chicken after a game.

Popson returned to his homestate in 1992, shortly after his basketball career ended. At first, the adjustment was hard. His first marriage broke up. He moved to Raleigh for a few years, then returned to Pennsylvania when his father died in 1998.

But Popson has found stability in his marriage to Holly—an accomplished photographer—and their beloved young daughter, Bella. The Popson family lives in a 100-year-old refurbished house back in his hometown of Ashley, Pennsylvania. The house once belonged to Popson's grandmother.

Popson has also found work that he likes with his job for the Pennsylvania Department of Corrections.

"I don't wear a uniform to work," Popson said. "Basically, I wear a whistle and an ID badge. It's interesting work. I do see a lot of these young kids coming in who really don't realize what they've done. It's disheartening sometimes. The war on drugs takes a lot of prisoners."

Popson got involved in his current job because his older brother, Jay, has also worked for the department for over 20 years.

"I've found out there are no secrets in jail," Popson said. "But that's okay. I have nothing to hide."

DAVE POPSON BY THE NUMBERS

5.7   CAREER SCORING AVERAGE AT UNC.

10.0   SCORING AVERAGE DURING SENIOR SEASON (1986-87).

14-0   CAROLINA'S REGULAR-SEASON ACC RECORD IN POPSON'S FRESHMAN AND SENIOR SEASONS.

23   CAREER HIGH IN POINTS, AGAINST MARYLAND IN 1987 ACC TOURNAMENT.

52.1   CAREER FIELD-GOAL PERCENTAGE AT UNC.

134   CAREER GAMES PLAYED AT UNC.

760   CAREER POINTS AT UNC.

SCOTT WILLIAMS

Triumph over Tragedy

Small things happened to Scott Williams over his basketball career that others might have taken for big things, nursing them with rage and allowing them to fester. For instance, Williams wasn't drafted at all after his college career ended at North Carolina in 1990. Also, Michael Jordan used to yell at him some when the two teamed together in Chicago. Of course Jordan yelled at everyone, trying to make his teammates better, but some guys really didn't take it well. And Williams sat on the bench for most of his 15-season NBA career, never averaging more than 7.6 points per game in any one season.

His college career featured some disappointments, too. For instance, he never got to play in a Final Four for the Tar Heels. But you know what?

So what!

Williams rebounded from an almost unfathomable family tragedy to play 15 years in the NBA, win three titles with the Chicago Bulls and settle down into family life in Phoenix along with his wife and two young children. He knows how blessed he is now, to be able to bookend his NBA career by playing with Jordan at the beginning and LeBron James—his high-flying teammate for the 2004-05 season with the Cleveland Cavaliers—at the very end.

"I'm having the time of my life," said Williams, who retired from basketball after the 2005 NBA season and will now pursue a career in sports broadcasting. "I'm only 37 years old. And I have another life waiting for me outside of basketball."

To talk with Williams is to enjoy a conversation with a man who is well-adjusted, smart, and doesn't take himself too seriously. That's remarkable, considering the news he received in the fall of 1987. Williams was a sophomore, coming off a strong freshman season for a team that went 32-4 and made it to

Robert Crawford

SCOTT WILLIAMS

1987-1990

Scott Williams (above) scored 1,508 points in a Tar Heel uniform, and says that "nothing comes close to the Carolina family." NBA teams ignored the 6-10 center in the 1990 draft, but he hooked on with Chicago and won three NBA titles playing alongside Michael Jordan. Williams (right) went on to carve out a successful 15-year career in the league.

Cleveland Cavaliers

the Elite Eight. On the morning of October 16, 1987, North Carolina coaches Dean Smith and Bill Guthridge had to tell Williams that his father, Al, had shot and killed his mother, Rita. And that his father then killed himself with the same gun.

"I can't think of a worse time for me than having to knock on Scott Williams's door (to give him the news)," Dean Smith said in our interview for this book.

The news of the murder-suicide shook Williams to the bone. His parents had been going through a tough divorce. Rita Williams had told some people she was afraid of what Al might do. Still, no one expected this.

For a day or so, Williams said, he thought about not playing basketball for Carolina that season.

"But it was great therapy to play," Williams said. "Playing was one of the few times when I could forget, when I didn't think about the fact that I had lost my parents. I know some people have to talk to somebody to work through their emotions. But for me, being on the court, running, having to concentrate on Coach Smith's defensive strategies—that demanded all my attention and focus."

Williams said he never would have made it through except for the support of the Carolina basketball family, including the basketball secretaries, his coaches, and his teammates.

"There were these difficult moments," Williams said. "I remember sitting in the dorm room, all alone, trying to grasp why it happened. But I always felt I had somebody I could call and go see a movie. I didn't necessarily want to sit and talk about it, but I didn't want to be alone. I wanted to see a movie. And not only were they all there for me, but they were there for my brother, too, who was three years older and just a regular guy. That's when I understood what 'family' meant. I was truly blessed as far as being in the right situation to deal with a horrific tragedy."

A few hours after the murder-suicide, Williams's uncle called Smith at 3 a.m. to tell the coach the news. Smith waited until 7 a.m. to call Guthridge and then asked his assistant and close friend to accompany him to Williams's dorm room.

"I needed the company," Smith said.

After telling Williams, Smith and Guthridge both flew to California within the next few days to help the family. Smith attended the funeral.

"That's the saddest thing I ever went through as a coach as well," Guthridge said. "For him to go through that and simply to survive and be a good person, let alone not getting drafted and then having a 15-year pro career—that's amazing."

Continued Guthridge: "Scott's mother was a beautiful, wonderful person and really sharp. We didn't pick up on anything unusual in the recruiting. They had a nice home and everything seemed fine. But when he was a freshman, she came and told us she was getting a divorce—that apparently Al had been abusive. And she started moving around and having to take out restraining orders and switching cars.

"I was out there in California the next fall, just a couple of weeks before it happened, looking at another player. While I was there, I stayed overnight and I took Al to an Angels game. I wanted to talk to him, and he seemed fine. He said all the right things: 'If she doesn't want me, I'll find someone else. I'm okay.' That sort of thing. Two weeks later, he killed her."

It would be wrong to shroud Williams's entire career at Chapel Hill in black because of the deaths of his parents, however.

"There is so much more to Scott," Smith said. "For one thing, he hits a golf ball about 340 yards."

Williams compartmentalized his life very well and didn't want people to treat him with kid gloves, then or now. He became an essential part of four straight Carolina teams, and most of his memories from Chapel Hill are happy ones.

Williams said he wasn't quite sure he could play at the college level until a 1987 game in the ACC tournament his freshman year against Virginia. In a game that noted college basketball writer John Feinstein would call in the next day's *Washington Post* "as memorable as any in the 34-year history of the ACC tournament," Williams played a key role. In the first overtime, the Tar Heels trailed by two points as Jeff Lebo dribbled upcourt and tried to get off a last-second three-pointer. The ball was slapped away from Lebo. Williams ended up with the ball about eight feet away, not facing the basket. He had no time to think.

"I threw up a baby hook, and it went in," Williams said, smiling at the memory. The Tar Heels would win in double overtime, 84-82.

Williams was also tangentially involved in one of the rare media firestorms created by Dean Smith. In 1989, Smith got upset during a game at Duke when Duke students teased Williams's teammate J.R. Reid by holding up signs and chanting: "J.R. Can't Reid."

In the press conference prior to that season's ACC tournament, Smith said he believed the sign and the chant constituted racial slurs. Smtih also said publicly that Reid and Williams (two black players) had a combined SAT score that was higher than Duke's Christian Laettner and Danny Ferry (two white players).

Smith has a near-photographic memory, and he had recruited all four players and knew all of their academic transcripts well. No one disputed the facts, but there was an outcry in Durham that the Duke players' privacy had been violated.

The Blue Devils and Tar Heels would then meet in the 1989 ACC tournament final in the game Williams now remembers more fondly than any other win he had at Carolina.

"The biggest win we had as a team was when we won the ACC championship," Williams said. "We had won the ACC regular-season title two years in a row, in my freshman and sophomore years, but then we won the ACC tournament [77-74] when I was a junior over Duke. I remember going back in the locker room, and since most of us were minors, there were no champagne corks to pop. So we got cans of Sprite, shook them up, popped the tops and sprayed them all over each other."

Williams had a solid career at Chapel Hill, but there was some question about his shoulder when he entered the draft in 1990 after his senior season. Nobody picked him. A number of teams wanted him to come to training camp, with no guaranteed contract. One of those was the Bulls. He thought he could make the team because of their average frontline, and he thought Jordan might keep an eye on him.

That was certainly the case. Williams got assigned the locker right next to Jordan. Said Jordan in 1992, discussing that assignment at the NBA Finals with *The Los Angeles Times*: "I wanted him next to me so I could hammer him."

Hammer him?

"Keep him in line," Jordan clarified.

MJ rode Williams, but he rode everybody.

"I had some verbal barrages," Williams said. "But the professionalism I saw in Chicago—from Jordan, Scottie Pippen, Bill Cartwright, and so many others—that helped keep me in the league for so long."

Riding Jordan's shoulders, the Bulls would win NBA championships in each of Williams's first three years in Chicago. Williams was a valuable reserve on each of those teams and got to find out that champagne sprays just as easily as Sprite does.

Williams went on to play for six other NBA teams. Along the way, he met his wife, Lisa, and they had their son, Benjamin (four) and their daughter, Ava (two).

"I wondered at the time in Chicago if anything in life could live up to that— three straight championships," Williams said. "I know now, though, having had the children, that the championships are in second place."

Of all the many great players Williams has played with in more than 800 career games, he said Jordan and LeBron stand out the most.

"Jordan would do things in practice that were just tremendous," Williams said. "He'd drop 30 on the Knicks in New York, take a long flight home to Chicago and still run the hardest and be the best player in practice the next day. Other superstars I've played with, when they play 40 minutes the night before, they are dogging it the next day.

"LeBron? He's just like Jordan in practice. And the other thing he shares with Jordan is they have an unnatural confidence. No matter the situation, they always expect to raise their game to the next level and to flat-out get it done, often in a way that can leave you awed."

Williams hopes to eventually get into radio or TV broadcasting. He has dabbled in that already, doing some WNBA broadcasts and some local TV and radio shows in Phoenix. He also won't rule out coaching, although he's concerned about the travel with his two young children.

"I'll satisfy my jones for the game in some way," Williams said, "but I also want to be around my children and see them develop. I want to always be there for them, just like Carolina has always been there for me."

SCOTT WILLIAMS BY THE NUMBERS

3   NBA CHAMPIONSHIP RINGS (ALL WITH CHICAGO).

4   THREE-POINTERS IN HIS UNC CAREER (VS. 591 TWO-POINTERS).

6.2   CAREER REBOUNDING AVERAGE AT UNC.

10.9   CAREER SCORING AVERAGE AT UNC.

11   REBOUNDS IN ACC TOURNAMENT TITLE-GAME WIN OVER DUKE IN 1989.

55.1   CAREER FIELD-GOAL PERCENTAGE AT UNC.

1,508   CAREER POINTS AT UNC.

PETE CHILCUTT

A Surprising Success

If they gave a prize for tallest marathoner, Pete Chilcutt would have won it. At six foot 10, Chilcutt has completed three marathons since he left Chapel Hill. Imagine that sight—a guy who weighs 230 pounds and is two inches short of seven feet, jogging down the street with all those 5-6, 130-pound whippets.

Chilcutt, 37, is one of those guys who likes to try new things and then usually has more success with them than one might expect. As a freshman at Carolina, he was unimpressive enough that he was one of the few non-medical redshirts Dean Smith ever had.

"For my first year or so at Carolina, my basketball future was going exactly nowhere," Chilcutt said.

But Chilcutt ended up being a first-round NBA draft choice and managed to stick around for nine years in the NBA. Chilcutt came off the bench in 90 percent of the games he played in his NBA career and never averaged more than 6.1 points per game. But he developed an accurate three-point shot in the pros—he ended up making 188 "threes" in his career—and was a fine practice player and teammate.

Chilcutt has now settled with his wife, Monique, and their two small children in California, where he is a financial consultant in the Sacramento area. Since his job is dependent on the stock markets, he puts in some unusual hours.

"I get up at 5:30 each morning, and I'm at work by 6:15 a.m.," Chilcutt said. "Once you do that for a little while, you get used to it. The markets usually close at 1 p.m. our time. Then I shut down shop around 3 p.m. or so and get out of here. It's something I enjoy; I'm basically my own boss, which is nice."

Chilcutt spent most of his formative years living near Tuscaloosa, Alabama. His stepfather was a professor at the University of Alabama, and his mother a teacher as well. Chilcutt played basketball for a small school in Eutaw, Alabama.

Robert Crawford

PETE CHILCUTT

1988-1991

In Pete Chilcutt's (above) first game as a freshman against No. 1 Syracuse, he scored 14 points, grabbed 13 rebounds and hit a jumper to send the game to overtime. The Tar Heels went on to win that game, and Chilcutt went on to score 1,150 points in his North Carolina career. Chilcutt (right) met his wife, Monique, while playing NBA ball in the Sacramento area, where Chilcutt now works as a financial consultant. They have a six-year-old son, Aidan, and an 18-month-old daughter, Isabella.

Courtesy of Pete Chilcutt

"It was a dream back then when I watched Carolina on TV," Chilcutt said, "but I never thought I'd play basketball in college. The summer after my junior year, though, the recruiting started getting pretty serious. I talked to Coach Guthridge about that time."

Remembered Guthridge: "The first time I saw him was at a Five-Star camp up in Pittsburgh. I really liked him. I think I got his home phone number from Howard Garfinkel. I called his mother, and she said, 'We've been waiting for your call.'"

It wasn't hard to convince Chilcutt to come to UNC—he was entranced by the thought of playing at the same school that Michael Jordan did. His family had even tried to send him to one of Carolina's basketball camps one summer, his mother told Guthridge, but it was full.

"When they offered me a scholarship, I was like, 'Are you kidding me?'" Chilcutt said. "And I had no idea what I was getting into."

Chilcutt came to Chapel Hill as a skinny freshman. He would eventually try to compensate for that by eating a lot of pizza, which wasn't exactly the right way to gain weight.

"When I got there, Joe Wolf, Dave Popson, J.R. Reid, and Scott Williams were all there, too," Chilcutt said. "There were guys all over the place in my position. Right before we played an exhibition, Coach Smith came up to me and said, 'Pete, I was looking at the depth chart. Would you consider a non-medical redshirt?' I agreed on the spot."

It was a wise move. Chilcutt needed the extra year to grow and mature. He would end up playing 140 total games for Carolina the following four seasons, from 1987-91, never missing a game. He still ranks among the all-time UNC leaders in that category. The Tar Heels made it to at least the Sweet 16 every year Chilcutt played and advanced to the Final Four when Chilcutt was a senior co-captain, along with Rick Fox and King Rice.

Among Chilcutt's favorite memories at Carolina were the 1987 Hall of Fame Tip-off Classic in Springfield, Massachusetts, against No.1 Syracuse, which was the first college game in which Chilcutt had ever played.

"I hit a pretty big shot in that one," Chilcutt said.

It was *really* big. As a redshirt freshman, Chilcutt and the Tar Heels were down 59-45 early in the second half to a Syracuse team featuring Rony Seikaly, Derrick Coleman, and Sherman Douglas. Chilcutt started and was playing a lot because Smith had suspended J.R. Reid and Steve Bucknall for the game due to an off-court incident. He ended up with 14 points and 13 rebounds, including a 10-footer at the end of regulation to send the game into overtime. The ball hit the left side of the rim and the backboard before finding the net, and Carolina ended up winning, 96-93, in overtime.

Said longtime Carolina radio play-by-play man Woody Durham: "I thought Chilcutt had a very good Carolina career. He wasn't an absolutely outstanding player, but Chilcutt gave us what we needed every time out."

The other bookend of Chilcutt's Carolina career—Game 140 of 140—came in the well-known 1991 North Carolina-Kansas Final Four semifinal. Smith, facing old assistant (and future Tar Heel head coach) Roy Williams, ended up getting ejected in the Jayhawks' 79-73 win. After the ejection, Smith walked down to the Kansas bench and shook Williams's hand, producing one of the few graceful acts on a difficult night for North Carolina.

"I was part of the reason for Coach Smith's ejection," Chilcutt said. "He got one of his technicals for arguing a phantom call against me." (The other came for leaving the coaching box.)

Chilcutt was selected late in the first round of the 1991 NBA draft, by Sacramento with the No.27 pick. He would spend the next nine years playing for seven different teams, almost all of them on the West Coast.

The best team he played on was in 1994-95 in Houston, where he came off the bench for a Rockets team that won its second straight championship behind Hakeem Olajuwon and Clyde Drexler. That team also featured former North Carolina point guard Kenny Smith.

"And that was back when 'Jet' still had some hair," Chilcutt said.

Chilcutt met his wife, Monique, while playing in Sacramento. They now have a six-year-old son, Aidan, and an 18-month-old daughter, Isabella.

At one point after his NBA career, Chilcutt thought he might want to teach. But once he started to pursue his certification, it didn't feel right. "I had some kind of epiphany and just walked out of the classroom," Chilcutt said. "I worried whether there was going to be enough money to support a family."

Instead, Chilcutt went into finance. He's been a financial consultant since early 2002. He remains in touch with the Carolina basketball family and attended a UNC game in late 2004, where he visited with Guthridge.

Chilcutt said he is rarely recognized in California.

"Mostly, it's just, 'Hey, who's the tall guy?'" Chilcutt said. "I tease my wife about the 'Chill Factor,' and that if she ever wants to realize the full effect of people recognizing me, we'd have to go back to Carolina. Who knows? Maybe we will one day."

PETE CHILCUTT BY THE NUMBERS

8.2   CAREER SCORING AVERAGE AT UNC.

25   CAREER SCORING HIGH, AGAINST VIRGINIA AS A SENIOR.

53.6   CAREER FIELD-GOAL PERCENTAGE AT UNC.

83   CAREER BLOCKED SHOTS.

GEORGE LYNCH

The Senior Who Couldn't Fail

Can a man make an entire basketball career out of doing the dirty work? He can, if that man is George Lynch, now a dozen years removed from the 1993 UNC national championship team. If you remember Lynch's game at Carolina—heavy on rebounds, steals, and guts—then you've still got him pegged.

Lynch has carved out 12 seasons in the NBA doing the same sort of things. He has never averaged more than 9.6 points in any NBA season. Yet he keeps sticking around because, at age 35, he will still dive on a loose ball, make an extra pass, and play hard defense.

"I've always been a team player who could tell my teammates, 'Okay, you're good, but we're trying to win trophies,'" Lynch said as we sat together in a Mexican restaurant in Charlotte. "I learned to play winning basketball at a young age."

Everyone associated with the 1992-93 Tar Heel team that won the national championship will tell you that Lynch was the heartbeat of that team. His teammates would later vote him team MVP of that season. The final four games of his career were all double-doubles in the NCAA tournament, as he averaged 17.5 points and 11.0 rebounds against Arkansas, Cincinnati, Kansas, and Michigan.

"He was a jewel for us," coach Dean Smith said of Lynch, "and just an unbelievable leader."

"On that 1993 team, Lynch was the glue," Dick Vitale said. "Never spectacular, always solid."

In this book, I have generally avoided writing about current NBA players with Chapel Hill pedigrees, since there's no mystery as to where stars like

GEORGE LYNCH

1990-1993

George Lynch (above) didn't miss a single game in his 140-game UNC career, and it's a good thing, as the Tar Heels needed the 12.5 points and 7.8 rebounds he averaged over the course of his collegiate career. Since leaving college, Lynch (right) has made an NBA career out of diving for loose balls, rebounding and playing defense—all the difficult basketball work that superstars don't always want to do.

Antawn Jamison, Vince Carter, and Rasheed Wallace have ended up. But I made an exception for Lynch. Having watched him on a regular basis in my Charlotte hometown while he played for the Charlotte Hornets (who would later move to New Orleans), I thought Lynch should be highlighted as someone whose work ethic, more than his talent, has made his long career in basketball possible. He plays basketball the way we all think we would play ourselves if we made the NBA.

In the pros, Lynch (6-8, 235 pounds) hasn't scored nearly as often as he did at UNC. But he has stuck around and even flourished—he started much of the 2004-05 season for the New Orleans Hornets—because of what he's willing to do.

"What I learned at Carolina has made me the player that I am," Lynch said. "Although teams do look for a superstar at this level, the superstar also has to have someone do the little things. I don't care about scoring 10 points or whatever. But you have some guys who say, 'I just want to score.' So you have to have someone like me to make them happy."

Lynch knows his NBA career is winding down rapidly, however. He had a severe case of plantar fasciitis last season, which meant that his right heel felt like someone was frequently jabbing a hot fork into it. He hopes to play a couple more years in the league, but knows that's not a certainty.

Lynch's home base is the Dallas-Fort Worth area, where he lives with his wife, Julie, son, Jalen, (eight) and daughter, Mia, (two), in the offseason. He plans to build a sports facility there (www.Mabasports.com for more details) with the help of some business partners in the DFW area. The facility would include football, basketball, and baseball training centers for kids.

"I'd handle the basketball, of course," Lynch said, "and teach the kids the Carolina way."

Lynch embodied the Carolina way about as well as anyone Dean Smith coached. Woody Durham, the team's longtime radio voice, recalled Smith's emotions when the 1993 national-title team held its banquet shortly after winning it all.

"Dean never speaks very long at those things," Durham said. "He started thanking people, and when he got to George he had to stop. He got very emotional. His last words were, 'He came to play every day.' By then it was obvious he was too emotional to continue, and he had to sit down."

Lynch's journey to Chapel Hill wasn't a straight path. He grew up in Roanoke, Virginia, "basically in the projects," Lynch said.

He was, in fact, lucky to grow up at all. Born two months premature, Lynch only weighed three pounds at birth. The doctor who delivered him originally pronounced him dead at birth, and although he wasn't, Lynch remained in an incubator for more than a month.

Lynch's parents were separated early. "But I did have a stepfather who was part of my life from age two to high school," Lynch said. "And my father was still around some."

Lynch, his friends, and his cousins would meet on a field in the middle of their apartments and run spontaneous track meets or play baseball with one bat, no gloves, and one tennis ball.

Always a good athlete, Lynch left his home as a high-school junior to move three hours away to Flint Hill (Virginia), a basketball powerhouse where he could live with the family of one of his teammates and showcase his skills for college scouts. During the first few months at Flint Hill, Lynch's father would come pick him up and take him back to Roanoke on every other Friday. On the Fridays that Lynch had to stay in Flint Hill, he would cry.

"But all that helped prepare me for Carolina," Lynch said. "In my junior year in high school, I pretty much said goodbye to my family and moved in with another family. When I got to school my freshman year, I wasn't homesick at all. I'd already been through it."

Virginia made a hard recruiting push to try to get Lynch, but he chose UNC primarily because he wanted to play in the Smith Center. He quickly proved his worth to the team. By the time he was a sophomore, UNC was in the Final Four, and Lynch was averaging 12.5 points and 7.4 rebounds per game.

But Duke won national championships in both Lynch's sophomore and junior years. By the time he was a senior, in 1992-93, he had a burning desire to win one for himself.

"I remember calling a meeting and saying there was going to be a mandatory running program," Lynch said. "And everyone had to lift weights. And everybody had to make a pact that there was going to be no drinking. And I think everybody bought into it. I didn't want to cut any corners."

Lynch wasn't all work and no play, though. Once, in front of his teammates at the beach, he took on all comers in an impromptu wrestling contest.

"It was so funny," Lynch said. "Well, it wasn't funny afterward, because I hurt my shoulder a little bit. Coach Smith got mad, and he said we couldn't do any more extracurricular stuff like that."

And he also has a fond memory of something that would probably be the basis for a reality-TV show today.

"I remember the pregame meal, after everybody finished eating, we would take everything that was left over and put it in a pitcher," Lynch said. "Everything. If it was on the table or under the table, you would mix it in. Then we'd see who would eat it. And Scott Cherry would take everybody's money every time."

Ultimately, that 1993 team would win the championship. It never would have been possible without Lynch. He and Derrick Phelps—who would finish their careers as UNC's top two all-time leaders in steals—trapped Chris Webber in the final seconds of the championship game. Webber, momentarily bewildered, called a timeout he didn't have. North Carolina got to shoot free throws because of a technical foul on Webber instead, icing the game.

If Lynch and Phelps hadn't cornered Webber (who should have been called for traveling earlier on the play but wasn't), the national title game might have turned out differently. But there's no place for Lynch's contribution on that play in a standard basketball boxscore. It was some more dirty work—just a little higher profile than usual.

GEORGE LYNCH BY THE NUMBERS

0   GAMES MISSED IN A 140-GAME UNC CAREER.

2   PLAYERS WHO HAVE LED UNC IN REBOUNDING FOR THREE STRAIGHT SEASONS (LYNCH AND SAM PERKINS).

11   IN FOUR YEARS, THE NUMBER OF THREE-POINTERS LYNCH MADE (COMPARED TO 711 TWO-POINTERS).

7.8   CAREER REBOUNDING AVERAGE.

12.5   CAREER SCORING AVERAGE.

241   STEALS, RANKING SECOND ALL-TIME AT UNC TO DERRICK PHELPS.

1,097   REBOUNDS, SECOND ALL-TIME AT UNC TO SAM PERKINS.

Where Have You Gone?

ERIC
MONTROSS

A Haircut and a Title

You know about the unmistakable haircut. You know about the 1993 NCAA championship he helped win for North Carolina. But there is much more you don't know about Eric Montross, one of the most interesting and talented players to ever come through Chapel Hill.

You probably didn't know that Montross's NBA career was ultimately ended by a baby gate, for instance. Or that he met a girl at the end of his freshman year in college and never wavered from her side—Eric and Laura Montross are now married and have two young children. Or that he was a speech communications major at North Carolina and has started a business where he does team-building and leadership seminars for corporations. Or that he and his family have now moved back to Chapel Hill, where Montross has started to team with Woody Durham as the color analyst on the Tar Heels' official radio broadcasts.

But we're getting ahead of ourselves.

When faced with a Goliath-like Montross—a seven-foot, 275-pound mountainous man—it's best to understand him in stages, from head to toe. Let's start with the head, then, and that famous flat top.

"Interesting story," Montross said in his deep, resonant voice as we sat together in a room inside the Dean Dome. "Back in Indiana in about eighth grade, my dad told me, 'You ought to get a flat top.'"

Scott Montross, Eric's father, wasn't someone to trifle with. He's been a successful lawyer for years, played basketball at Michigan and is six foot eight himself. But Eric argued, relenting only when his father agreed to get his hair buzzed as well.

"So I go in, get mine cut—and he bailed," Montross said, laughing.

Nevertheless, Montross quickly grew to like his new 'do.

Robert Crawford

ERIC
MONTROSS

1991-1994

Eric Montross (above) was a bit of a legend as a college player thanks to his flat top, his "00" uniform and his tenacity on the court. He ranks seventh all-time in rebounding and fifth all-time in blocks at UNC. Montross (right) retired from the NBA after a foot injury and now does some corporate speaking as well as his new job as the color analyst on the Tar Heels' official radio broadcast.

"At that age, everyone wants to look cute for the girls," Montross said. "That was the age of hairspray and combing it all the time. When I finally got rid of all that I was like, 'That's the best thing I've ever done in my whole life! I can wash it with a washcloth. I don't have to blow dry anything.' Plus, I think it helped my aerodynamics."

Montross grew up in Indianapolis, the son of Scott and Janice Montross and older brother to Christine (now a talented writer and med-school student). Eric was the latest—and biggest—in a line of college basketball players. His grandfather, John Townsend, was a 6-4 All-American at Michigan, a superb passer known as the "Houdini of the Hardwood." While Townsend was several decades ahead of his time, Eric's game seemed several decades behind. He was a bruiser. A worker. A grinder. He never was particularly graceful, but he could throw in a jump hook over anyone, and he was remarkably consistent and even-tempered.

Montross smiles a lot more now than he used to when he was getting pounded on constantly by smaller, lighter opponents. But even in college it's hard for anyone to remember a time when Montross lost his cool. That could be because Montross was always a smart guy. If you move slightly down from the flat top, you'll find a big brain. And he's witty as well as smart.

In one North Carolina media guide, he said his favorite book was the second volume of the *Encyclopedia Brittanica*. This so impressed the excellent *Sports Illustrated* writer Alexander Wolff that he once wrote most of a magazine piece about Montross using encyclopedic terms from *Brittanica's* Volume 2, only to find out after his research that Montross was just goofing off on the questionnaire.

Montross didn't goof off much of anywhere else.

"I wasn't the most athletic or talented guy," Montross said. "But the work ethic my dad instilled in me made me want to run in the morning before school or get there early and practice for an hour with my coaches before class. My parents never pushed me to the point I was turned off by basketball, but they gave me a heartfelt, generous chance to get better."

Montross was the best big man in the country in high school, where he won a state championship at Lawrence North back when Indiana still had the no-class system popularized by the movie *Hoosiers*.

"Hoosier high school basketball is like Texas high school football," Montross said. "It's phenomenal. In eighth grade, I signed my first autograph. I thought it was so cool."

Since he lived in Indianapolis and had so much family history at Michigan, folks thought that either Michigan or Indiana (coached then by Bob Knight) would get him. But Montross chose North Carolina instead, angering the local populace but pleasing another portion of his body.

"When I decided to come here, it was a gut feeling," Montross said. "It was one of those pit-of-the-stomach feelings that tells you when something's right."

By the time he was a sophomore, Montross was already becoming somewhat legendary, both for his "00" uniform and his tenacity. In one two-point win over Duke in his junior season, Montross scored 12 points, grabbed nine rebounds, and blocked three shots while bleeding from two different cuts on his head.

Said TV commentator Dick Vitale: "I'll never forget that night. That was in 1992, against Christian Laettner and Bobby Hurley and the team that ultimately won the national championship. Montross was scratching and clawing that night. He was a total warrior that night, man, a total warrior. He starts bleeding from his head. He comes out. He goes back in the game. The crowd is going wild. And the Tar Heels win."

Former Tar Heel coach Bill Guthridge agreed: "That game has always stood out for a lot of fans. Duke was good. We were good. And here was Montross—playing hard for us like he always did. Now if you had blood on you like that, they'd get you out of the game, probably, but that time they didn't, thank goodness."

The Dookies took Montross personally. The Duke student newspaper once ran a huge blank space and captioned it thusly: "This big useless white space was put here to remind you of Eric Montross."

Montross was far from useless, of course. He had a drop step, a jump hook and an absolute unwillingness to be moved out of the post. His haircut also made him something of a cult hero at Chapel Hill. Many members of the pep band got a Montross "high and tight" buzz cut before the 1993 Final Four in New Orleans.

In his junior year, Montross was first-team All-ACC, and North Carolina (34-4) won the national championship. Montross scored 16 points and had five rebounds in that 1993 title-game win over Michigan.

"Everyone remembers the timeout," Montross said, referring to Chris Webber's famous blunder that cost Michigan a chance to tie the game late. "I guess I get a little bit defensive because people say, 'Well, that really won it for you guys.'

"Well, that really didn't win it for us. It certainly helped etch it in stone. But that's almost pawning off responsibility to a mistake. Our team had just this magical ability to trust in each other, and not care about who got the most accolades. There were no contracts involved. It was just a pure form of basketball where people loved playing and wanted to do it for each other. I've never been on a team that was closer than that one."

Montross has a couple of other fantastic memories of Chapel Hill. For one, it was the place he met his wife, the former Laura Leonard of Lexington, North Carolina.

"Laura was a year ahead of me in school," Montross said. "The first time we really got to know each other, we both had an exam the next morning. But we sat in a room, talking and talking, until 4:30 in the morning. It was one of the best nights of my life. A lot of people can't believe that anybody would meet somebody during their freshman year and never break up with them—but we did. We've had 10 years of marriage that has been magical. She's the best wife and mother I've ever been around."

Montross also remembers vividly North Carolina's comeback from 20 points down with 9:21 to go against Florida State during the national championship season of 1993. It happened in the Dean Dome, a place that FSU guard Sam Cassell had derisively labeled a "wine-and-cheese crowd" the year before. Cassell was woofing in the locker room at halftime that a "white boy," Henrik Rodl, couldn't guard him.

But Rodl started a frantic comeback with a three-pointer in the second half. The crowd was on its feet, screaming and thrilled, for the final minutes. Florida State disintegrated under a flurry of North Carolina three-pointers and steals, and the Tar Heels won, 82-77.

"We were always taught to never watch the scoreboard and just focus on our job," Montross said. "I remember that whole run—Brian Reese, George Lynch, Donald Williams, Derrick Phelps, Henrik Rodl. All of it. What a game."

After his senior year in 1994, Montross was a first-round draft pick of the Boston Celtics. He traversed most of America and Canada over the next 10 years, playing for Boston, Dallas, New Jersey, Philadelphia, Detroit, and Toronto. He mostly came off the bench during an unspectacular but solid career, playing in 465 games and averaging 4.5 points and 4.6 rebounds.

"I'm real positive about the whole thing," Montross said. "I got to play against Tim Duncan, David Robinson, Shaq, Hakeem Olajuwon, Patrick Ewing....I just wish I could have played more."

And now we come to the bottom part of this seven-footer—his feet. In his final NBA season, Montross was at home in Toronto, a few hours before the game, when the unfortunate happened.

"We had a baby gate crossing the second or third stair going up to our bedroom," Montross said. "So I stepped over it, as any parent would do instead of taking down the baby gate every time. It was not a misstep. It was not a trip. But when I stepped off my left foot, I felt what I thought was just a foot cramp."

That foot cramp turned out to be far worse. Montross would ultimately see nine different specialists trying to get his size-19 foot healed, but it never really has.

"The analysis is that the step was the straw that broke the camel's back," Montross said.

He would retire because of the injury, and he still feels a burning sensation in his left foot most every day.

"The fact is it ended my career and I'll probably live with it for the rest of my life," Montross said. "But I think there may be a greater purpose for me. I'm still very fortunate to have the career I did, and most people would give their foot for a 10-year career in the NBA."

Montross now spends lots of time with his kids—seven-year-old Andrew and five-year-old Sarah. He also runs a nonprofit basketball camp in Chapel Hill each summer, with all of the proceeds going to a local children's hospital. He's only 34 and not sure what the next few years will hold for him. But he plans for now to stay in Chapel Hill with his family, doing some motivational speaking, and his radio work, and seeing where life leads.

"I've had an amazing ride," Montross said. "I know I'll stay close to basketball in some capacity, but I can't wait to see what the future will bring."

ERIC MONTROSS BY THE NUMBERS

6.8   CAREER REBOUNDING AVERAGE.

11.7   CAREER SCORING AVERAGE.

16   POINTS IN CHAMPIONSHIP-GAME WIN OVER MICHIGAN IN 1993.

19   MONTROSS'S SHOE SIZE.

58.5   CAREER SHOOTING PERCENTAGE.

139   CAREER GAMES AT UNC.

169   CAREER BLOCKED SHOTS.

Where Have You Gone?

BRIAN REESE

Reese's Pieces

H ave basketball, will travel. And travel. And travel.
For eight years following his career at North Carolina—where he started at small forward for the 1993 national championship team—that has been Brian Reese's motto. Well, one of his mottos. Another one he had to adopt overseas was "No pay, no play." Sometimes owners' checks can have a little problem clearing the bank in Europe or Asia. Reese was a firm believer that only his shoe soles, not his checks, would be made of rubber.

Rarely, though, has a former North Carolina player stayed overseas longer or enjoyed it more than Reese. He would go anywhere to play, cheerfully chasing money and basketball in places like Japan, Korea, Australia, Austria and France. He's been paid in euros, yen, and Taiwanese dollars.

"I've had a great time seeing the world," Reese said.

Whether overseas or in America, Reese has never stopped chattering on the court. When Dean Smith used to tell his team to speak up and help each other, especially on defense, he would often add, "All I'm hearing is Brian out there!"

Now Reese is back in the States, living in Charlotte. In August 2005, he began a new job as an assistant high-school basketball coach and teacher at Porter Ridge High, just outside of Charlotte. Reese also dreams of a mental-health clinic of his own one day.

Said Reese: "I want to have a program area for at-risk kids, handicapped kids—basically any kids who need services. I eventually want to have my own facility."

Reese also occasionally teaches at local basketball camps, trying to inculcate kids into what he and so many other former lettermen call "The Carolina Way." Reese is well-versed in it, of course. And of all the players I talked with for this

Robert Crawford

BRIAN REESE

1991-1994

Brian Reese (above) averaged 11.4 points per game for the 1993 NCAA champion Tar Heels. Today, Reese (right) lives in Charlotte, where he is an assistant high-school basketball coach and hopes to one day run a mental-health facility for children.

book, Reese seemed to know the most among the former players about where his contemporaries currently live and work. It helps that he's naturally gregarious and has his mobile phone always at the ready.

If you threw a name out there like Donald Williams, Reese would rattle off: "I think he's playing in the CBA for a team somewhere way out west. Maybe Idaho? Joe Wolf is his coach. Joe used to be a college assistant, you know, but now he's doing that." And sure enough, a later check reveals Reese is exactly right. In the spring of 2005, Wolf was the coach and Williams one of the players for the CBA's Idaho Stampede.

Now 34, Reese has a nine-year-old son, Brian Jr., who lives with his ex-wife in the New York area. He sees his son every month. Reese lived back up in his homestate of New York for a couple of years after retiring from basketball, running another program for kids that was somewhat similar to the one he hopes to start in Charlotte.

Reese is an incurable optimist. We sat together and talked in Charlotte while watching North Carolina play at Wake Forest on TV. The Tar Heels trailed nearly the whole game, but Reese kept saying, "I'm not worried." Eventually, Wake Forest won, which only made Reese declare: "That'll be the last time they beat us this season."

As a child, Reese learned quickly that he had to talk fast to get a word in edge-wise. Growing up in The Bronx, he was the youngest of 10 children. His brothers and sisters used to call him "Baby Blue" as a kid, since that was so often the color in which his mother would dress him.

A standout baseball and football player as a kid, Reese barely touched a basketball until he was 11 or 12 years old. Suddenly, he hit a growth spurt, which made others say he should start playing basketball. He already had a favorite team by then. The first basketball game Reese ever watched on TV, at age 10, was the classic 1982 Georgetown-North Carolina NCAA final. Fred Brown, who would ultimately throw the ball directly to James Worthy when Georgetown had a chance to win, was a friend of the Reese family.

"The rest of my family was watching because of Fred Brown," Reese said. "I was the only one in the room rooting for Carolina, and I was only rooting for them because of their colors."

"Baby Blue" had found himself a team. But he had no idea how to play the game.

"I didn't know how to dribble or anything," Reese said. "But when I was about 12, they put me in this local tournament because I was so tall, and the coach told me, 'Just rebound.' But I'd walk with the ball and turn it over, and you know what happens when you do that in an urban community—when you're out there playing and you're not any good? They taunt you. People were screaming at me, calling me names, embarrassing me."

Determined to stop the taunting, Reese started going daily to the park near his house. He had natural athletic gifts, and when his work ethic kicked in, he suddenly became one of the best young players in the country.

"Brian was one of those young phenoms," recalled Bill Guthridge, who helped recruit Reese to North Carolina. "He was one of the best players in New York City as a high school freshman, and by that time he already could really dunk."

Reese joined North Carolina's vaunted recruiting class of 1990, which also included Derrick Phelps, Pat Sullivan, and Eric Montross. All four of them played key parts in North Carolina's 1993 championship season. That was Reese's junior year at Chapel Hill, and his best. He made the cover of *Sports Illustrated* after scoring 25 points in a game at Florida State and had numerous acrobatic dunks. But he's also remembered for the dunk that missed—in the NCAA tournament that season against Cincinnati.

In an Elite Eight game, North Carolina stormed back from a 15-point first-half deficit to tie the game. The Tar Heels ended up with the ball under their own goal with the score tied and 0.8 seconds remaining. Dean Smith drew up a superb play that used Montross as a decoy and actually called for a lob to Reese. Smith told Reese that he would be wide open and to just catch the ball and guide it into the basket while in the air.

It worked perfectly—except for one thing. Phelps lobbed to Reese, who caught the ball directly in front of the basket. Instead of guiding the ball in, however, Reese came down, gathered himself for a game-ending dunk, jumped—and missed the dunk entirely. Overtime.

"Phil Ford actually went on the floor and rolled head over heels when Brian missed that shot," remembered Woody Durham, the longtime radio voice of the Tar Heels.

"Everyone remembers that shot," said Reese. "I was watching a quiz show one time and a question about it was on there. The reason I tried to dunk it was because all through my career, that's what I had done. I see it up there, I'm dunking it. There wasn't going to be none of this 'Just put it in.' I don't know how to just put it in! I know how to dunk! But the guy undercut me, I missed the dunk and boom, new game!"

Thankfully for Reese's legacy, the Tar Heels won anyway, and Reese went on to have a great 1993 NCAA tournament. His 27 assists over six games were only one less than Phelps, the point guard, had during the same period. In the national title win over Michigan, Reese had eight points and five rebounds.

His senior season, though, was a disappointment. Reese was bothered all season by an ankle injury sustained in preseason practice. The injury was serious enough that Smith advised Reese to redshirt and come back the following year. But Reese decided to play through it. He wasn't the same explosive player, and partly because of that he could never crack an NBA roster.

"I was thinking about everything else but my health," Reese said. "Still, I had a great career after college. I have really liked going everywhere and seeing everything while playing overseas, and I've got a lot more I want to do with my life."

BRIAN REESE BY THE NUMBERS

3.3   CAREER REBOUNDING AVERAGE.

4   OFFENSIVE REBOUNDS IN NATIONAL FINAL AGAINST MICHIGAN IN 1993.

8.3   CAREER SCORING AVERAGE.

11.4   SCORING AVERAGE ON 1993 NATIONAL TITLE TEAM.

18.7   SCORING AVERAGE IN 1993 ACC TOURNAMENT.

25   CAREER HIGH IN POINTS.

50.5   CAREER FIELD-GOAL PERCENTAGE.

Where Have You Gone?

SCOTT WILLIAMS

Son of the Coach

For a young man with a common name and a famous father, Scott Williams seems quite sure of his own identity. Williams, 28, works for Wachovia Bank in Charlotte as a bond trader. He has carved out his own identity at the bank's headquarters, trading billions of dollars worth of bonds for Wachovia's institutional clients.

Yes, he is the son of current North Carolina coach Roy Williams—and quite proud of it. He will gladly discuss any moment of the Tar Heels' run to the 2005 national championship. Yes, he's also quite aware that a much taller Scott Williams—also featured in this book—played a lot more for the Tar Heels in the late 1980s and also crafted a fine 15-year NBA career. No, this Scott Williams is not worried about any of that. The only thing Williams worries about much on weekends is whether North Carolina wins—he makes the 150-mile drive from Charlotte to Chapel Hill quite frequently—and whether world events somehow inversely impact the $100-200 million of inventory he's holding in his job at the bank at any given time.

Williams was a walk-on, five-foot-10 point guard at North Carolina who made the varsity and was put on scholarship his senior year by coach Bill Guthridge. He scored five points in his varsity career—exactly five more than his father ever scored.

"If we were up 30 with 30 seconds to go, that was my time," Williams said.

The smart money probably had Scott Williams following father Roy's footsteps and becoming a coach after he graduated from Chapel Hill in 1999. Scott had grown up around college basketball and was a gym rat from birth.

"It's always been this way for me," Williams said. "If someone's dad was a normal dad and then became a big movie star, there would clearly be a 'before'

SCOTT WILLIAMS

1998-1999

Scott Williams (above) only scored five points during his Tar Heel career—but that's five more than his dad, Coach Roy Williams. Williams (right) and his wife, Katie, were married in August 2005. Williams considered entering the coaching profession like his father but went into finance instead. He now works for Wachovia Bank in Charlotte as a bond trader.

and an 'after.' For me, my dad has always been a head coach since I've been aware of what was going on. I've always been a coach's son."

But while Williams loves talking strategy with his father and going to Chapel Hill for his mother Wanda's home cooking and his father's home games, he decided not to enter the coaching field.

"You have to have something of a chemical imbalance to want to coach for a living," Williams said, laughing. "Pops definitely qualifies. I don't have that yet. I love the *idea* of being a coach. But it's such a non-stop, intensive job. I also love the fact that when I leave work on Friday afternoon I don't think about work."

Roy Williams said in an interview for this book that it was fortunate that Scott didn't try coaching. "I'm still alive because of that," Williams said, laughing. "If Scott had come home and said he wanted to be a coach, his mother would have shot me first, then him."

Scott still takes basketball very seriously, though. On March 6, 2005, just before halftime of what would become a thrilling, 75-73 UNC win over Duke, Williams actually got thrown out of his second-row seat in the Dean Dome by referee Larry Rose. Scott was angry that Duke coach Mike Krzyzewski was in Rose's ear for quite a while after Coach K got upset about a substitution he hadn't been allowed to make.

Said Scott: "I never cursed. But I did keep saying, over and over: 'Larry Rose, be a man! Coach K owns you!'"

The words apparently struck a nerve with Rose, who ordered Williams to be escorted from his seat. He had to watch the rest of the game elsewhere.

Scott does still keep in shape by playing basketball, and he obviously inherited some of his father's organizational qualities. He hosts what he cheerfully refers to as the "Scott Williams Invitational." Each Monday night at 9 p.m. in Charlotte, Williams rents out a local church gym and invites a bunch of former college basketball and football players he knows to play pickup ball.

"We've never had an argument," Williams said. "We basically have a tryout for new guys. They get to play with us once, and I ask two or three guys what they thought. If the guy was calling sissy fouls or arguing or wasn't in good shape or didn't pass the ball, he doesn't come back."

Married in 2005 to the former Katie Wolford, Williams enjoys living the life of a successful urbanite. He has bought his first house, just two miles from downtown Charlotte.

It's ironic that Williams does well in the banking business when his job is making financially educated guesses, since he can't seem to predict his own family at all. He thought his father would leave Kansas the first time North Carolina offered its head-coaching job (in 2000) and then that he would stay the second time (in 2003).

"I was 0-for-2," Williams said.

Scott Williams was named for legendary North Carolina star Charles Scott, also featured in this book.

"My freshman year at Carolina was Charlie Scott's junior year at UNC," Roy Williams recalled. "I thought I was pretty good, and then I found out there were about another 10 levels higher than where I was. Charlie was on the varsity and a very pleasant guy, and then when the games started he did some of the most amazing things I had ever seen. I liked the name 'Scott' anyway, but I also wanted my first-born son to remind me of amazing basketball."

Scott Williams spent most of his formative years in Lawrence, Kansas, where Roy was then the head coach at Kansas. Roy Williams would often try to schedule his team's one off day a week around Scott's high-school and college basketball schedule so that he could see his son play. Roy Williams chartered a plane to get to Scott's "Senior Day" at UNC in 1999, sending his Kansas team ahead to Iowa State, telling them he would see them the next day and then watching Scott start against Duke.

What kind of father is Roy to Scott and his sister Kimberly?

"I was always the kid in high school who had the absolute strictest parents," Scott Williams said. "Hands down. But I think that's the product of his core family values. Every time he was at home, we had to sit down and have a family dinner together. And in high school, that ended up getting more in my way than anything else. I wanted to go out and play pickup ball at the outdoor courts every single night. But when he was in town, that wasn't happening."

Said Roy: "I didn't get a chance to do a lot of things other fathers do, because I was gone so much. But whenever I was home, I got up with Scott and Kimberly every morning and made them breakfast and we'd talk. It wasn't a nutritious breakfast—toast or Cheerios or something. But it did give us some time together."

Scott Williams grew used to being around the Kansas basketball players, who would come to the family's house to eat breakfast on many Sunday mornings. "In exchange, they'd go to church with us," Williams said.

As a player, Williams teamed with another future UNC player and one of his best friends, Brad Frederick, on a team that won the state championship. "I was anything but a high-school stud," Williams said. "I played a fair amount, but I was just the backup point guard."

Said Roy Williams: "I'm proud of what Scott accomplished in basketball, but I'm 100 times prouder of all the work he did to get there. He didn't have a lot of natural athletic gifts—I mean, look at his father."

Although Scott Williams loved Kansas and his family, he decided to go far away for college. He applied only to Arizona State and North Carolina.

When he got to Chapel Hill, he tried out for the junior varsity team, made it, and played there for two years. Phil Ford was the coach. As a junior, Williams tried out for the UNC varsity. He didn't hold out much hope of making it, but he did.

Said Bill Guthridge, the coach of that squad: "He earned it. I didn't put him on because of who he was. He was a good player and a good ingredient for us. What you want in a walk-on is someone who will bust his tail in practice and represent you well off the court."

Said Scott: "I will never, ever be able to pay Coach Guthridge back for what he did for me by putting me on the team."

Scott Williams played sparingly in 33 games over the next two seasons. When he scored for the first time, on an old-fashioned three-point play against Florida State in 1998, Roy and Wanda were watching on satellite TV in Kansas. Within minutes of the basket, Dean Smith left Roy Williams a congratulatory message on his home phone.

Scott also got to enjoy the ride to the Tar Heels' Final Four berth in 1998, led by Antawn Jamison, Shammond Williams, Vince Carter and Ed Cota.

Incidentally, if you've followed the Tar Heels the past few years, you know that a number of Williamses have followed Scott Williams to Chapel Hill. In fact, Williams is now the most popular surname in UNC basketball history, recently surpassing Smith. Jawad, Marvin, Shammond, Donald, and two Scott Williamses have all played for the Tar Heels.

As for Roy's son Scott, he's quite happy in Charlotte.

"The trading floor at Wachovia is young," Williams said. "It's not a place where people usually stay forever, because it's very stressful. But it's a meritocracy. And I love it."

SCOTT WILLIAMS BY THE NUMBERS

1   TIME THE ACC CENSURED WILLIAMS AND HIS RESERVE
         TEAMMATES BECAUSE THEY WERE ACTING "TOO EXCITED" ON
         THE BENCH.

5   CAREER POINTS AT UNC (WHICH REPRESENTS FIVE MORE
         THAN HIS FATHER).

6   WILLIAMSES WHO HAVE PLAYED AT UNC (IT'S THE MOST
         POPULAR LAST NAME IN TAR HEEL BASKETBALL HISTORY).
         SMITH IS SECOND WITH FIVE.

9   CAREER ASSISTS AT UNC.

33   CAREER GAMES AT UNC.

JOSEPH FORTE

Trying to Get it Back

In Matt Doherty's mind, three players stand above the rest in North Carolina basketball history when the game is tight and the seconds are few. The three men Doherty would like to take the final shot in that situation who have worn Tar Heel blue are Michael Jordan, Rashad McCants, and Joseph Forte.

That's just one man's opinion, of course, but it's an interesting one. Doherty and Forte had their conflicts in Chapel Hill. But Doherty knows firsthand how good Forte was during his brief, two-year career in Chapel Hill. Forte was the scoring leader of Doherty's first team at North Carolina—the 2000-01 squad that won 18 games in a row, rose to No.1 and eventually finished 26-7 with a second-round loss in the NCAA tournament.

"Joe was one of the most talented players I've ever coached," Doherty said. "He was a true competitor who really had a knack, just like Jordan and McCants, to be very calm and confident in big-time situations. He was not afraid to take—and to make—big shots."

But Forte's career careened into the rocks shortly after he left North Carolina and Doherty after his sophomore season in 2001. Forte was named co-Player of the Year that season, along with Duke's Shane Battier, and was a first-team All-American at shooting guard with a 20.9 scoring average. At age 20, he became the first-round draft pick of the Boston Celtics. Little has gone right since then for Forte, however. He had problems with coaches, teammates, and the police in the ensuing four years. He now believes he should have stayed in school for four seasons.

"Basketball-wise, I was ready to go early," said Forte, who is now 24. "Emotionally, I was not....I've been a basketball wonder for some time now, but has my attitude been a wonder to be around?"

JOSEPH FORTE

2000-2001

Joseph Forte (above) set a scoring record as a freshman after averaging 16.7 points per game. He then topped that mark as a sophomore, averaging 20.9 per contest. He turned pro after that year, but quickly fell out of favor in the NBA. In 2005, Forte (right) was trying to make it back into the NBA by playing for a minor-league team in Asheville.

In my role as a sports columnist for *The Charlotte Observer*, I drove to Asheville in early 2005 to visit Forte. At the time, he was coming off the bench for the Asheville Altitude, a minor-league pro basketball team in the NBA's developmental league. I wanted to write a story about Forte's rise, fall, and attempt at a career resurrection, and I did that for the January 25, 2005 editions of *The Charlotte Observer*. The information gathered for this chapter came partly from that visit. Forte agreed that I could also write about his experiences for a chapter in this book to serve as something of a cautionary tale. I'm grateful for his honesty and forthrightness.

In Asheville, I found a young man who had been chastened by his first experience in the NBA—he had washed out of the league after two controversial seasons—and wanted badly to make amends.

"I was an All-American," Forte said as we ate lunch together at an Asheville restaurant. "And then I was a guy who had gotten arrested. That defines my life, right there. That's how up and down it has been."

Now 24, Forte has been in the national spotlight since he burst onto the scene at Chapel Hill as an 18-year-old freshman. He had played in the shadow of current NBA player Keith Bogans in high school at DeMatha High in Maryland, but emerged quickly in college. Winning a starting job in preseason practice under coach Bill Guthridge, Forte knocked in a three-pointer on his first collegiate shot. He was an instant success, with his baby face, unstoppable mid-range jumper and a jersey number (40) that was a subtle nod to his last name.

"I really liked Joseph and never had any problems with him," Guthridge said. "I think the world of him and think he can play. The last year I coached, when he was a freshman, he was great and did everything we asked him to do."

Forte had a higher scoring average that season (16.7) than Phil Ford, Jordan or anyone else ever had as a freshman at Chapel Hill (McCants has since surpassed it). Forte was the ACC's Rookie of the Year and a guiding force in the Tar Heels' surprising run to the 2000 Final Four, where they lost to Florida in the national semifinals.

"Coach Guthridge basically was a father figure to me," Forte said. "He was good to me. When people started giving him a hard time toward the end of my freshman year, that became a cause for me to play even harder for."

Guthridge retired after the 2000 season at age 63.

"Even at the Final Four that season, I thought I would coach until age 70," Guthridge told me in an interview for this book. "But in the next six weeks, I was only home two nights. And, kind of like Dean did, I hit the wall. I thought, 'If you can't give 100 percent, you're going to go down fast.' So I decided to retire."

The Tar Heels unsuccessfully tried to hire Roy Williams (he would change his mind three years later, on attempt No. 2) and ended up hiring Matt Doherty, the hard-charging Notre Dame coach who had played on the 1982 North Carolina national championship team. Forte adored Guthridge, but Doherty was another story.

"I came in and brought about change at a rapid pace," said Doherty, who would last only three seasons in Chapel Hill. "Maybe if I was more subtle with change, it would have had a better impact not only on Joe, but on the whole program. I understand the dynamics of the situation better now. To go in and institute change in a more subtle manner would be better for everyone involved. That is a lesson I've learned."

Doherty gave Forte even more of a green light on the court than Guthridge had. But Forte said their relationship was jagged.

"It wasn't all bad, because we were winning," said Forte. "But we didn't understand each other. We didn't communicate very well."

Some of Forte's teammates that season also had problems with him, believing he shot too often. Forte—while acknowledging that his only close friend on the team his sophomore season was Julius Peppers—called this "a sibling rivalry." Forte also said that Doherty yelled at him a good bit that season in practice, and that occasionally he would yell back at his coach.

Said Doherty: "I was trying to hold Joe to a level of accountability that any coach would expect from their players. Work ethic. Unselfish play. I was very direct and honest at times, and maybe that was different than what he was used to."

Forte had some unbelievable games in his sophomore season. The one he remembers most fondly was the 24-point, 16-rebound effort against Duke that paced an 85-83 win at Cameron Indoor Stadium. Forte's 16 rebounds set an all-time UNC record for rebounds by a guard, showing the world that he wasn't simply a scorer.

After the season, Forte decided to go pro. He said in our interview that financial security for his family was a key issue, and also that Doherty's aggressive coaching was a factor.

Doherty said, though, that he was basically told by a number of people close to the program when he was hired in July 2000 that Forte would probably go pro after his sophomore season.

"That's why I signed Jackie Manuel so fast," said Doherty, who had obtained a commitment from Manuel within days of being hired. "I was aware we were going to need another '2' guard."

Doherty, who remains close to many at North Carolina despite his turbulent coaching tenure there, also said he was rooting for Forte to make a basketball comeback.

"I wish Joe Forte nothing but the best," Doherty said. "It'd be a great, unbelievable story if he got back to the NBA."

It will be a difficult road for Forte, because his first shot at the NBA produced a lot of controversy.

"The years at Carolina were my golden years," Forte said. "And then in the pros, the main problem was I just wasn't playing, and I didn't know how to handle it. I didn't control my emotions. I understand that I was wrong."

The Boston Celtics drafted Forte in 2001 with the 21st overall pick and signed him to a three-year guaranteed contract worth about $3.2 million. They wanted to make him a point guard, figuring like many other NBA teams that a slender, 6-4 shooting guard might get too banged up and have trouble creating his shot in the NBA.

Forte didn't want to be a point guard, though.

"They were looking out for my future," Forte said, "but I didn't get it. All I could think of was I was an All-American as a shooting guard, and now they want me to do something that I have to learn from scratch."

Once Forte realized he wasn't going to play much, he started to anger the Celtics. He would show up late for practices or wear a throwback jersey of another NBA team, like the Celtics' longtime rival L.A. Lakers.

"Joseph was used to being the best," Guthridge said. "And when he wasn't, he just didn't handle that right."

After one season, the Celtics happily shipped Forte to Seattle. But the change of scenery didn't help. Forte, struggling with his ball-handling and stuck as a third-string point guard behind Gary Payton and Kenny Anderson, started to pout. He would tease his teammates at the wrong time. Once, after a Seattle loss in which Forte didn't play, he started gleefully singing in the shower: "What goes up, must come down ..." Sonics teammate Jerome James became so angry that he went after Forte, trying to hurt him. No one was ultimately injured in the scuffle, but the Sonics' response to the incident told you all you needed to know about their feelings for Forte at the time. They didn't punish James at all, but they suspended Forte for a game and fined him $11,000.

In April 2003, back in Maryland, Forte got in trouble with the police. In a 65-mph zone, he was stopped for going 90 mph. During the traffic stop, police also found marijuana and a pistol in Forte's car.

"I was a person basically trying to escape reality," Forte said. "And I felt alone. I felt like I needed protection. I thought someone might try to take a shot at me. I had to call my mother from the jail. It was embarrassing."

The Sonics wanted to get rid of Forte, but no one was going to trade for him at that point. They ended up waiving him, paying him the final million of his contract just to stay away. And Forte did just that, laying low for about 15 months. He stayed with friends and family in Washington, D.C., and New York. He said he saved most of his money. He contemplated going overseas to play.

But because money wasn't a problem and he hoped to get back into the NBA as quickly as possible, he took a job in Asheville instead. On the night I saw

Forte play, only about 500 people were scattered throughout Asheville's ancient Civic Center, watching the game. (The team would fold just months later.)

"Is it embarrassing? No," Forte said of the crowd. "What's embarrassing are some of the things I did—some of my bad behavior. I mean, I've been arrested. So I can't look at a crowd and go, 'There's not enough people here.'"

Forte has tried to reconnect with his alma mater recently. He didn't go anywhere near the basketball office while Doherty was still coaching (although Doherty said he would have greeted him warmly). But in early 2005, he drove back to Chapel Hill for a cleansing visit and lunch with Guthridge and Dean Smith.

"Hopefully Joseph has hit rock bottom and he's going to grow from all of this and have a nice NBA career," Guthridge said. "I think the world of him. I just wish I could have helped him more through all this adversity."

If Forte doesn't make it back into the NBA long-term, he said he would like to start some sort of "inspirational foundation" to help young people. And he understands that he may not make it back.

"I just want to know I did my part," Forte said. "I've already had my dream, you understand? I made it to the NBA. And now I have to dream a new dream, which is to succeed in the NBA and to be a professional. I can't be mad at my life. I'm just happy to get another opportunity."

JOSEPH FORTE BY THE NUMBERS

16   REBOUNDS AGAINST DUKE AS A SOPHOMORE, SETTING A SCHOOL RECORD FOR REBOUNDS BY A GUARD IN ONE GAME.

16.7   SCORING AVERAGE HIS FIRST SEASON (THEN A UNC FRESHMAN RECORD).

20.9   SCORING AVERAGE AS A SOPHOMORE, WHEN HE SHARED ACC PLAYER OF THE YEAR HONORS WITH SHANE BATTIER.

23.7   FORTE'S SCORING AVERAGE IN ACC GAMES AS A SOPHOMORE.

81.0   CAREER FREE-THROW PERCENTAGE.

1,290   POINTS IN TWO-YEAR UNC CAREER. IF FORTE HAD MAINTAINED THE SAME PACE AND STAYED FOUR SEASONS IN CHAPEL HILL, HE WOULD HAVE SURPASSED PHIL FORD FOR NO. 1 ON THE UNC ALL-TIME SCORING LIST.

Where Have You Gone?

JULIUS PEPPERS

Dunk of a Lifetime

Julius Peppers is the only man on the planet who has played in both the Super Bowl and the Final Four. Guess which one he thinks is a bigger deal?

"The Final Four," Peppers said. "Especially in North Carolina. I know that's kind of hard to believe, but it's real. The Final Four means a little more."

Peppers, 25, should know. He's one of the few athletes who has never had to leave his home state to obtain a scholarship or a job. Peppers grew up in Bailey, North Carolina, played both football and basketball at North Carolina, and then went on to a seven-year, $50-million contract with the Carolina Panthers as a defensive end.

After being chosen with the No. 2 overall pick in the 2002 NFL draft, Peppers has become one of the finest and most breathtaking defensive players in the NFL. He made his first Pro Bowl in 2004, as a starter for the NFC, and was an ESPN staple thanks to plays like a 97-yard interception return and a 60-yard fumble return against Michael Vick for a touchdown. The Panthers also let Peppers dabble as a wide receiver near the goal line in 2004. He never caught a pass, but he received so much respect that he sometimes was double-teamed in the end zone.

Atlanta Falcons coach Jim Mora has mused aloud about signing Bill Walton so that he can guard Peppers on such plays in the future.

"Peppers scares me," Mora said. "He is an unbelievably, athletically talented human being."

Said Panthers teammate Mike Minter, who has played alongside Peppers at strong safety since Peppers entered the NFL in 2002: "I can tell you right now, if everything stays the same and he doesn't get hurt, 'Pep' will be seen as the best

Robert Crawford

JULIUS PEPPERS

2000-2001

This dunk against Wake Forest was Julius Peppers's (above) favorite play during his UNC basketball career. He scored 21 points in his final collegiate basketball game in the 2001 NCAA tournament, before choosing to focus solely on football. Peppers (right) is now one of the elite pass-rushing defensive ends in the NFL and played in his first Pro Bowl in 2005.

Ron DeShaies

defensive lineman to ever play the game. We'll say when he retires that we won't see anything like that again for the next 50 years."

Peppers lives in Charlotte now, where he's a regular at home games for the NBA's Charlotte Bobcats. He gets his basketball fix that way and by watching the Tar Heels on TV or in person whenever he can. He makes the pilgrimage to Chapel Hill a couple of times every year for home games.

Basketball was Peppers's favorite sport as a kid. That makes sense for someone who was named for Julius Erving, and who grew up only 55 miles from Chapel Hill. Peppers thinks that he might have been able to make it in the NBA, too. But football scouts drooled over him so insistently that Peppers gave basketball up after two seasons for the Tar Heels—Bill Guthridge's last and Matt Doherty's first.

"I had a love for basketball, and I still do," Peppers said. "North Carolina basketball was such a great tradition to be part of—what a great family."

Peppers's two-year basketball career paralleled that of Joseph Forte, who was one of his closer friends on the team. While Forte had serious issues with Doherty's hard-nosed coaching style, Peppers never did. Still, in Peppers's final season in Chapel Hill as a redshirt junior, he played football only.

"I knew at some point I'd have to pick one or the other, and it was going to come to an end," Peppers said. "Me not coming back as a junior didn't have anything to do with Matt Doherty. I liked him as a coach. He was always good to me. I heard things about stuff he said to other players, but he never said anything bad to me. It was about making a career decision, about doing what was best for me at the time."

Peppers (6-6, 283) retains some great memories of Chapel Hill. It is the place where he started to overcome his inherent shyness (one of his former roommates said Peppers never spoke his entire freshman year). It is also the place where he became the physical sixth man on the 2001 Final Four team coached by Guthridge.

"He was a godsend for us," Guthridge said. "We had some injuries and some illness with our big men that year, and all of a sudden Julius comes out there after football is over and just keeps getting better and better. Julius was really fun to coach. Never said 'Boo'—just brought his lunchpail to work every day.

"And his hands?" Guthridge continued. "I can see why the Panthers are lining him up at wide receiver occasionally. He has unbelievably great hands. We've had a lot of big men with good hands, but Peppers and Bobby Jones— they had super-duper hands. Throw it anywhere and they'd catch it."

Chapel Hill is also the place where he converted one of the most thunderous dunks in Dean Dome history.

"Peppers was such an explosive player in the air," Forte said. "But that dunk....Oh, man! What he did to that ball to turn it from a regular alley oop to a *tomahawk*. That was amazing."

Let Peppers tell you more about the dunk, which came against Wake Forest in the Dean Dome on January 6, 2001. It's still his favorite play that he ever made on a basketball court, and a good ice-breaker if you ever happen to run into Peppers at a cocktail party.

"They were undefeated," Peppers said. "It was close all the way. In the second half, they turned it over and there was an outlet pass. It got away from Ronald Curry [Peppers's teammate in both basketball and football] and he couldn't really catch up to it. But I'm running! I'm filling the left lane. And he barely saves it from going out of bounds and at the last minute he saw me.

"I'm like, just throw it up there! *Throw it!* And *boom*—he threw it. I caught it with both hands and slammed it down. I mean ... *I slammed it.* The place just went crazy."

The dunk tied the game at 55-all, and Wake Forest coach Dave Odom called a timeout to quiet the crowd. During that timeout, the noise never stopped, because Peppers's dunk was shown six consecutive times on the replay screen.

"Coach Doherty was trying to talk to us in the timeout, but the replay kept showing, and nobody was listening," Peppers said. "Everyone was chillin', just looking at the replay. Finally he stopped talking and watched it, too."

The Tar Heels ended up winning, 70-69.

Peppers was raised by his mother, Bessie Brinkley. Peppers's father supplied his name—Julius Frazier Peppers, with the middle name a tribute to boxer Joe Frazier—but not much else. He and Peppers know each other but don't have much to do with one another.

Always big and surprisingly graceful, Peppers starred in football and basketball as a teenager at Southern Nash. The Tar Heels recruited him to play both sports, although his scholarship came out of the football allotment. One of the legendary stories about Peppers came from high school, where he was so good that both his football and basketball jerseys were retired. Once, after a three-hour football practice as teammates sprawled on the ground in exhaustion, Peppers began doing back flips down the football field.

In full pads.

For so long, Peppers was so athletically dominant that it would surprise him when someone could hang with his every move. It still surprises him on a football field. Most NFL teams don't even try, content to double-team Peppers on every pass play.

In college basketball, though, Peppers came to the realization that he would finally be challenged every day from an athletic standpoint.

"When you get to the ACC, you realize quickly that those guys can really play basketball," Peppers said. "It was an eye-opener when I first got on the team."

It didn't take long before Peppers became a fan favorite, however. The students would yell, "Sack him, Julius!" while Peppers would body another player into a bad shot or clear everyone out under the boards to snare a rebound.

Peppers was redshirted as a freshman as the football coaches tried to figure out where to play him. They simply listed his position at the time as "athlete." When they decided on defensive end, Peppers led the country in 2000 with 15 sacks. He became the first unanimous All-American in football at North Carolina since Lawrence Taylor in 1980.

His Final Four experience came in 2000 as well, when Guthridge's final team made an unexpected run to win the South Regional. The Tar Heels lost in the national semifinals to Florida, 71-59.

"The Final Four was kind of like my first *big* game," Peppers said. "I had played in big games before, but not like that. That was fun. I was looking up in the stands and seeing Muhammad Ali and John Wooden. That was great."

The following year the Tar Heels would win 18 straight games and be ranked No. 1 under Doherty, but falter late in the season. In the NCAA round of 32, the Tar Heels were upset by Penn State. Most of the Tar Heels played one of their worst games of the season that day. But Peppers played one of his best, with 21 points and 10 rebounds.

Peppers flirted with the idea of also playing basketball the following year, in 2001-02. He had been good enough to make usually reserved basketball announcer Billy Packer gush on-air about his "Charles Barkley potential." With Forte turning pro, it's quite likely Peppers would have been the best player on the team. But he knew his future was in football, and he made the right move not to risk millions of dollars due to a basketball injury. Doherty's squad floundered without him, though, going 8-20 and starting rumbles of dissatisfaction among the alumni that would become an earthquake one year later.

Peppers burst into the NFL in 2002, being named the Defensive Rookie of the Year after getting 12 sacks in only 12 games. His totals would have been higher, but he was suspended for four games for taking a banned supplement containing an Ephedra-like substance. Peppers told me once in an interview we did for my *Charlotte Observer* newspaper column that he was offered the substance during his rookie year by a "friend" he met in Charlotte. He thought that the pill was legal and that it would give his tired legs some help.

"I made a mistake," Peppers said.

Peppers now is almost paranoid about what he puts into his body. He generally drinks only water, apple juice, and orange juice at restaurants, and only if they come to the table unopened, with the original seal intact.

In 2003, Peppers's second season, the Panthers made the Super Bowl and lost a thriller to New England. In 2004, at age 24, Peppers had his best season yet. But the Panthers faltered, going 7-9 after being beset by injury.

Although Peppers still occasionally watches an NBA game and wishes he could test himself in that league, he knows that he made the right choice. He believes he can become the most dominant defensive player in the NFL. And many people in the league do, too.

Kansas City head coach Dick Vermeil once called Peppers "a larger Deacon Jones."

Said Minter, his teammate: "On a scale of one to 10, as far as Pep's potential, I'd say he's probably at four or five right now."

If Peppers ever makes it all the way to 10, he may do a few things he even likes as much as that dunk against Wake Forest.

JULIUS PEPPERS BY THE NUMBERS

1   PRO BOWL APPEARANCE IN NFL (FOLLOWING 2004 SEASON).

3.7   CAREER REBOUNDING AVERAGE IN BASKETBALL.

5.7   CAREER SCORING AVERAGE IN BASKETBALL.

15   MOST SACKS PEPPERS POSTED AT UNC IN A SEASON, ONE SHY OF LAWRENCE TAYLOR'S SCHOOL RECORD.

21   POINTS SCORED IN HIS FINAL COLLEGIATE BASKETBALL GAME, IN THE 2001 NCAA TOURNAMENT AGAINST PENN STATE.

30   SACKS IN FIRST THREE YEARS IN THE NFL FOR CAROLINA PANTHERS.

60.7   CAREER FIELD-GOAL PERCENTAGE AT UNC.

ACKNOWLEDGMENTS

Like most buckets scored by a North Carolina basketball team, this book is a collaborative effort. If I were on a basketball court, I'd have a lot of pointing to do to show my gratitude for all the assists necessary to make this book a reality.

Thanks so much to Steve Kirschner and Matt Bowers, the North Carolina sports information gurus for men's basketball. Despite my innumerable requests in the middle of UNC's national championship season in 2004-05, they were, as always, trusted friends and absolute pros. Kirschner, the associate athletic director for communications at UNC, runs that department. And it's as good as any sports information department in America. Almost all of the "back-in-the-day" pictures in this book come courtesy of UNC, and I appreciate all of the photographers who snapped those for the university's archives.

Thanks to former North Carolina coaches Dean Smith and Bill Guthridge for grasping quickly what this project was about, embracing it, and spending so much time with me to ensure that I got it right. Thanks to current North Carolina coach Roy Williams for not only helping me out with a thoughtful interview smack in the middle of his championship season, but also for fathering a fine son, Scott Williams, who became one of the 35 players I devoted a chapter to for the book.

Thanks to everyone at *The Charlotte Observer* (www.charlotte.com), the wonderful place where I work, for allowing me to pursue this project on my own time and for being supportive of my work at the newspaper for all these years. All of those folks, especially my boss, Mike Persinger, are as fine as they come.

Thanks to all those writers who came before me with books I have enjoyed about the Tar Heels, Coach Smith and the basketball program. Art Chansky, Barry Jacobs, Ken Rosenthal and David Scott, among many others, have done some outstanding work in this department. Chansky's *The Dean's List* is a must-read for any North Carolina fan. Smith's memoir *A Coach's Life*, written with John Kilgo and Sally Jenkins, is superb. The coach's follow-up book, *The Carolina Way*, is also enlightening.

Thanks to photographers Robert Crawford, Ron DeShaies, and Michael Hughes for allowing me to use some of their excellent work in these pages.

Thanks to all those PR folks in the NBA who helped me locate players and information, including the Charlotte Bobcats' Scott Leightman and B.J. Evans; the New Orleans Hornets' Harold Kaufman; and the staffs of the Cleveland Cavaliers, Indiana Pacers, L.A. Lakers, Miami Heat and Washington Wizards.

Thanks to Patricia Porter of the NBDL's Asheville Altitude; Craig Pinkerton at the University of Tennessee; Steve Goldberg; and the PR staff of the Carolina Panthers.

Thanks to my Mom, who long ago hardwired a love of reading the newspaper into me. She's also a great babysitter. Thanks to my Dad, whose love of reading books made me want to write some. Thanks to my entire family and my wife Elise's entire family for their support, personally and professionally.

Thanks to all those who have contributed in some way to my website—www.ScottFowlerSports.com.

Thanks to all 35 of the North Carolina players who entrusted me with their stories. As Dean Smith would tell you, they are all equally exceptional.

And a special thanks to all the fans of Tar Heel basketball. If not for you, this book would not exist. I hope you enjoy it.